Praise for *Tarot for One*

"Courtney Weber is one of a new generation of Tarot authors who are making the cards fresh and relevant to today's world. Filled with real life examples, this book is almost like being in class with Courtney or like joining her in a fun and insightful conversation. She answers questions about the reading process as soon as (or just before) they arise in my mind. It's an updated Tarot for yourself packed with exciting new ideas and perspectives that I'll certainly be using."

—Mary K. Greer, author of *Tarot for Your Self* and *Understanding the Tarot Court*

"Most Tarot readers agree: reading Tarot cards for others is a snap compared to reading for yourself. Remaining objective is hard, especially when you are emotionally invested in the outcome. Thanks to Courtney Weber's *Tarot for One: The Art of Reading for Yourself,* you're not going to struggle any longer! With smart exercises, clever spreads, easy-to-understand interpretations and tons of examples, Weber provides the perfect framework for getting out of your own way and uncovering clear, unbiased answers. If you love Tarot and have always wanted to be able to read your own cards, this invaluable guide belongs on your shelf."

—Theresa Reed, author of *The Tarot Coloring Book*

"Filled with practical tips, real-life examples, and plenty of creative activities, *Tarot for One* will help you become your own best reader . . . as well as make you a better reader in general. Weber's firm yet gentle touch will guide you to find truth in the cards and within yourself."

—Barbara Moore, author of *Your Tarot Your Way*, *Tarot Spreads*, and the *The Steampunk Tarot*

"The enchanting Courtney Weber understands Tarot's exceptional power to tell the stories. She knows the most profound tale the Tarot will tell is the story of you. *Tarot for One* shows the reader how to find their story in the cards while staying grounded, avoiding pitfalls, and having fun."

—Sasha Graham, author of *Tarot Diva* and *365 Tarot Spreads*

"Tarot learning with a personal touch! *Tarot for One: The Art of Reading for Yourself* is riddled with incidents that bring the cards up close and personal. Weber has harnessed traditional correspondences and clearly voiced them in a tone that makes for a user-friendly study of the cards."

—Gina G. Thies, psychic advisor and speaker, author of
Tarot Coupling: Resources and Resolutions for Relationship Readings, and the
forthcoming deck, *Tarot of the Moors*

TAROT

FOR ONE

The Art of Reading for Yourself

COURTNEY WEBER

WEISER BOOKS

For Tiffany

This edition first published in 2016
by Weiser Books, an imprint of
Red Wheel/Weiser, LLC
With offices at:
65 Parker Street, Suite 7
Newburyport, MA 01950
www.redwheelweiser.com

ISBN: 978-1-57863-595-5

Library of Congress Cataloging-in-Publication Data
Names: Weber, Courtney, author.
Title: Tarot for one : the art of reading for yourself / Courtney Weber.
Description: Newburyport : Weiser Books, 2016. | Includes bibliographical references.
Identifiers: LCCN 2016032944 | ISBN 9781578635955 (7 x 9 tp : alk. paper)
Subjects: LCSH: Tarot.
Classification: LCC BF1879.T2 W388 2016 | DDC 133.3/2424--dc23
LC record available at *https://lccn.loc.gov/2016032944*

Cover design by Jim Warner
Cover images: spotlight background © Saibarakova Ilona / Shutterstock;
tarot card © natis76 / Shutterstock

Tarot card images of the Waite Deck created by Red Wheel/Weiser, LLC.
Interior by Kathryn Sky-Peck
Typeset in Raleway

Printed in Canada
MAR
10 9 8 7 6 5 4 3 2 1

*The Tarot embodies symbolical presentations of universal ideas,
behind which lie all the implicits of the human mind, and it is in this sense
that they contain secret doctrine, which is the realization by the few of truths
imbedded in the consciousness of all . . .*

—Arthur Edward Waite

CONTENTS

ONE

WELCOME TO THE "SELF-READ"

For over half of my life, I have enjoyed a deep love affair with Tarot. Tarot makes me laugh and cry. It brings me joy. It drives me insane. I shuffle, riffle, and deal daily, yet those first cards still incite as much curiosity and awe as they did in my first reading many years ago. I know that I am not alone. The fascinating power of Tarot continues to draw people in, as it has for centuries.

Whether you are new to Tarot or are reading this book to hone established Tarot skills, you are part of a glorious tradition spanning over six hundred years. For centuries, Tarot has been consulted for answers about love, personal purpose, money, or forecasting future events. Before Tarot was the accessible commodity that it is now, a *querent* (a person seeking a reading) would need to find someone to read Tarot for them. Not so anymore. With the accessibility of today's Tarot, reading for yourself is not only possible but in many cases preferable. I consult other readers a few times a year, but my primary Tarot reading is for myself.

Self-readings can structure individual reflection time. If we are mentally chomping on a particularly grueling issue, drawing even a single Tarot card can help us work through the situation. Seeing a reader for these questions can be helpful, but sometimes the cards will have a message that only we can decipher for ourselves. Reading our own cards is a good way to cross-check or confirm readings we've received from other readers.

Other times, a personal or spiritual need requires us to work things out, alone. If we read for others, experience in reading for ourselves grants us greater insight. Lastly, reading for ourselves is a solid way to learn Tarot.

As many readers will attest, reading for yourself can be difficult. In many of the classes I've taught, excellent readers lament, "I can read Tarot for others, but I just can't read my own cards." This encouraged me to start a class called "Tarot for One: The Art of Reading for Yourself." Because of its popularity, I wrote this book.

Tarot for One is designed to help you discover your own system of relating to the cards. The chapters will include traditional interpretations of Tarot images, but it is important that you remain open to your internal responses. Smothering personal responses by clinging to traditional meanings (for example, "This Tarot book says this card means progress, but my situation is definitely not progressing . . . my interpretation must be wrong") makes the work of self-reading extremely challenging, if not impossible. Approach the work with an open mind to your personal associations with the cards.

Know this: Tarot needs to learn your system of association more than you need to learn its system of symbolism. Through this book, you will have the opportunity to discover your own association systems and share them with the cards, creating a unique language for you and the cards alone.

To Begin, What Is Tarot?

Tarot is a deck of seventy-eight cards. Forty are numbered and bear a resemblance to playing cards commonly used in the Western World. These are broken down into four suits commonly titled Cups, Wands, Swords, and Pentacles. Sixteen of these are Court cards—Pages, Knights, Queens, and Kings—which are somewhat reminiscent of the Jacks, Queens, and Kings of Western playing cards. The remaining twenty-two are Trump cards known as the Major Arcana. Designs, themes, and titles for these different suits and for the Major Arcana will vary from deck to deck, sometimes wildly, as Tarot is a magnificent vehicle for artistic expression. Some decks refer to Wands as Staves or the Page as a Princess or otherwise. But the commonality among all Tarot decks is that there will always be seventy-eight cards total: fifty-six making up the four suits and their Court cards, and twenty-two comprising the Major Arcana Trumps.

Tarot cards depict characters, situations, and influences common to the human experience. When they are shuffled and dealt, they tell stories. These stories may be in response to a particular question. Some may give an overall view of a querent's life, like how a meteorologist might give the weather forecast. Readings might provide clarity about a confusing situation, explaining things that might otherwise be enigmatic. They may be used for *divining* (telling the future) or for providing insight into a past event. Other readings, particularly readings for the self, may be a way to reflect on a troubling issue or serve as a meditative exercise.

Tarot provides a bit of Magick in a world that can seem devoid of it. It is spiritual and interfaith, drawing from many religious traditions. It is beautiful; a deck's artwork alone is often worth its cost. But of all of Tarot's gifts, one of its greatest is being a powerful tool of self-reflection. Learning to read your own cards is a skill. Once you are able to do so comfortably, it is a brilliant way to develop an additional layer of self-awareness, understand personal needs, assess situations, and cultivate a deeper relationship to Spirit—however you know Spirit to be.

Where Does Tarot Come From?

Tarot's history is nearly as mysterious and complicated as its images. Some have suggested that the word Tarot is derived from an Ancient Egyptian word *ta-rosh*, meaning "the royal way," or that Tarot came from the Hebrew

Torah, meaning "law (of God)."[1] Other stories suggest Tarot originated in India and was brought through Europe and the Americas by the Roma people.[2] Robert Place, in *The Tarot: History, Symbolism, and Divination,* suggests that Tarot descended from the word *tarocchi,* a name for a deck of cards with a trumps suit that may have been named for the Taro River in Northern Italy, possibly an area of a paper industry at one time.[3] For all its mystical beginnings, it's likely that Tarot developed from practical roots: via a literal paper trail to China, when pulp made from the bark of the mulberry tree was used to make a substance that could be flattened, painted, and cut without crinkling.[4] Unlike earlier parchments such as papyrus, mulberry bark held its shape when cut and was durable enough to withstand repeated use. Through this technology, paper cards were born.[5] One legend suggests that paper cards were invented in 1120 CE for the amusement of an emperor's concubines.[6] Over several centuries, papermaking and playing cards moved through Asia and the Middle East, and as they did, more card images and games developed.

Tarot as we know it has its most direct roots to cards produced in Italy in the fifteenth century CE, when twenty-two Trump cards were added to playing cards already in existence.[7] It's possible that the Trumps were based on characters as recognizable to their contemporaries as Disney heroes and villains are to us today. The images are straightforward, without any of the symbolism found in modern decks. Most images reflected the lifestyle of the time, and wealthy people sometimes commissioned artists to depict specific family members in a personal suit of Trumps. Some historians believe that Tarot was originally only a trick-taking card game and was not associated with fortune telling or the occult until the end of the eighteenth century.[8]

The expense of the era's hand-painted cards kept Tarot relegated to the parlors of the rich, who could afford to produce them and possibly pay the authorities to look the other way when dealing them at society parties. Gambling and its accoutrements (playing cards, dice, etc.) were routinely banned in Europe. In part because of their general inaccessibility, Tarot cards took on a deep mystique.[9]

In the nineteenth century, the occult world became fascinated with Tarot and was determined to unlock its supposed ancient secrets. Decks began appearing from the workshops of artistically inclined occultists, inspired by images of ancient Egypt, Christian Gnosticism, and the Kabbalah. In the early twentieth century, a ceremonial magician named Arthur Edward Waite teamed up with esoteric artist Pamela Coleman Smith, herself a ceremonialist, to create a Tarot deck that would become the most influential deck in circulation today. Like its predecessors, this deck was created with the intention of returning mythic esoteric symbolism to Tarot. Yet, because of Smith's artistic ingenuity and the clarity of the symbolism within the cards, it has enjoyed a powerful mainstay in the Tarot world and inspired hundreds of other decks (including one that I created with a friend a few years ago). For decades, the deck was commonly known as the Rider-Waite, Rider being the publisher and Waite the creator. In recent years, Smith's name has been added to the deck, and it is now being called the Rider-Waite-Smith, or simply the Waite-Smith.

This book will primarily reference the Rider-Waite-Smith deck (which I will call the RWS deck). You do not need this specific deck to do the work, but you will need one that follows the basic premise of twenty-two Major Arcana (or Trump) cards and fifty-six Minor Arcana cards broken down into some variation of Cups, Swords, Wands, and Pentacles. Some variations of the Minor Arcana include chalices or vessels for Cups, scimitars or knives for Swords, staves or rods for Wands, coins or disks for Pentacles, or a different combination.

How Does Tarot Work?

A thing has power because it is given power. Paper money may be only a mixture of wood pulp, cotton, linen, or some other combination, but its worth is determined by its culture. If that currency were dropped from the air to an uncontacted tribe in the Amazon rainforest, it would have no value except maybe as fodder for a fire or as bath tissue. Yet, this does not mean that money's power is an illusion. For a long enough time people have placed faith that paper money holds the value it is assigned. Modern Tarot cards may only be petroleum-coated layers of paper pulp, but they contain power because they have been revered with it for centuries. This does not mean that only those who believe in Tarot will have a profound experience, although belief certainly helps. I have read cards at many a party and for many an unbelieving guest who approached my table "for fun" only to walk away amazed and/or frightened—and, often, a true believer.

Tarot works because it reflects a well-trod human journey. It is decorated with familiar characters and situations. Through them, we see ourselves. We are able to look at our lives spread before us in the way a picture book on myth and lore might describe the story of a hero. It gives us the opportunity to look at our choices and reflect on the potential outcomes, be they positive or negative. This is the explanation I give in interviews, and 75 percent of the time that's true. Yet, regularly enough (truly, about a good 25 percent of the time), Tarot reminds me that it is a beacon to the unknown and can tell us things we had no way of previously knowing.

A few years ago, I read for a friend I hadn't spoken to in quite some time. I designated one part of the reading as "worries and concerns." When I dealt the cards, the Emperor and King of Pentacles, which I see as fatherhood cards, both landed in that area. I asked my friend if he was worried about his father and he said no. He had spoken to his father only the day before, and all was fine. I shuffled and dealt again. This time, different cards I also associate with fatherhood landed in the "concerns" section. I apologized to my friend and told him I must not be having a good Tarot night. Later that week, however, he emailed me to say that his father was diagnosed with cancer the day after our reading. The disease had not been on his mind, yet Tarot knew.

It would be easier to say Tarot is only a pack of parchment with six hundred years of human investment and that it's more like an inkblot test than an oracle, solely giving us a reflection of our unconscious minds. But for me and so many other readers, moments like the one above happen too often to label them all as coincidence. Tarot holds a blessed mystery. Maybe someday neuroscience will explain the deep roots of prophetic Tarot readings, but for now there is enough pragmatism in the world. Tarot preserves some of the Magick.[10]

How Accurate Is Tarot?

Accuracy varies. Sometimes, querents will approach Tarot with explicit questions in mind: Who will I marry, and what day and year will I meet them? Exactly how many children will I have, and when will they be born? Will I be hired at this new job? And if so, exactly how much money will they offer me?

These questions are tough, because although Tarot can tell you if love, money, and family are likely to be in your future, it is difficult to garner dates, names, or salary figures from the cards alone. Hoping for such specific answers can leave a person feeling as though Tarot is not accurate at all. In general, deeper experience and familiarity with Tarot will ultimately offer quite accurate readings about the overall course of life's events. Our readings are most accurate when we are open-minded about their potential outcome, knowing Tarot can and will offer specifics about events to come (such as if serious love is in your future) but won't be able to offer minute details (such as your future spouse's hair color).

Is Tarot 100 percent accurate all of the time? Of course not! But neither is the weather forecast. Just as weather patterns change when affected by winds and tides, our destinies are also affected by the choices we make. Sometimes, Tarot will show us what *could* be instead of what *will* be. Sometimes, Tarot is far more on point than we can imagine, and cryptic readings can turn out to be uncannily accurate.

How Is a Self-Read Different from Other Readings?

When we read Tarot for others, we focus solely on their issues and concerns. When we read for ourselves, we focus solely on us. We do not have a seasoned reader present to help us make sense of the cards. *We* must be that seasoned reader, oracle, and conduit of the answer we seek. Some people consult the cards when they are working through a difficult situation. Others may consult them as part of a daily spiritual routine, in the same way that someone might read the Koran, the Torah, or the Bible. A daily spiritual routine is good for the mind and soul in the same way exercise and nourishing food are good for the body. In an age when many people are finding less satisfaction in the texts of mainstream faiths, Tarot provides both an anchor and a portal for the soul. It can keep us grounded while also allowing our souls to explore even deeper regions.

For those of us who wish to read Tarot for others, reading our own cards provides a deeper connection to the images, which ultimately increases our ability to read for others.

Why Would I Want to Read My Own Cards?

There are benefits to reading your own cards and seeking out other readers. Seeing another reader gets us out of our heads. We learn about the cards from other readers' associations. Seeing a reader can provide insight that is safely separate from our personal projections.

However, seeing someone else for a reading isn't always optimal. Sometimes, well-meaning Tarot readers lacking self-awareness can project their own issues onto a reading. It is for this reason I don't often read for my closest friends and family. As experienced as I may be, I still find it difficult to separate what I want for them from the reading's true message.

In general, readers want to give honest and helpful insight; and in the hands of a talented or experienced reader, that is what you will receive. But there is always a chance that you will end up seeing an ethical reader who just isn't having a great reading day. Readers get tired. Sometimes, even if they don't have a personal vested interest in you or your choices, the situation you are asking about may trigger something in them. It can be hard for me, as a reader, to keep from projecting my personal history onto people I see as making mistakes similar to those I have made myself. For many a young woman weeping at my reading table about a flakey boyfriend, I've wanted to wipe all the cards from the table, give her a big hug and a slice of cheesecake, and make her pinky swear that she'll never text that lazy bastard again. Yet, it's not my mistake to make. Even if a situation rings eerily true to my past mistakes, my job is to read the cards, not to be an armchair life coach! But while I can set the intention to put my own feelings aside for the sake of the reading, I know I won't always succeed. I am human, and therefore I will periodically screw up and project my own rabid issues onto others' readings.

Reading for ourselves removes the risk of a reader projecting their stuff onto our readings. Moreover, reading your own cards is more logistically and economically feasible. Most readers require an appointment and fee. If you have a burning question about, say, how your proposal will go over in tomorrow's staff meeting, you could see if a Tarot reader will squeeze you into their schedule . . . or you could pull out the deck and see for yourself! I actually keep a deck at work in the event I should need an answer at a moment's notice.

Why Is It So Hard to Read My Own Cards?

Tarot and mirrors share the same role: they reflect truth. Tarot reflects who we are, what we're doing, and where we're going. But our personal projections, like the projections from other readers, can make this truth difficult to decipher. When we peek at the mirror before heading out the door, our personal projections may only allow us to see large pores, acne, or scars. We may think the mirror's sole purpose is to remind us that we don't look the way we'd like. But on a different day, we may love the mirror. It shows us the laugh lines, the bright eyes, the things about our faces and figures that make us unique and beautiful. In truth, if a mirror were conscious and verbal, it probably wouldn't be concerned about whether we like what we see in its glass. Instead of saying, "Beautiful God/ess!" or "Nasty, foul creature!" the mirror would probably say, "You have kale in your teeth and a little cat hair on your pants." It might also say, "Your eyes are brighter when you wear purple." The mirror's role is not to flatter us, but simply to give us information about things we may want to clean up, adjust, or accentuate before we head out the door. It is our own projections onto the mirror that cloud its work.

Tarot's role is the same. It has had many purposes over the years, from parlor entertainment to occult studies to therapy, but its true calling is to show us the symbolic kale in our teeth or which personal choices best suit us. The tricky part is setting aside our personal criticisms or ego inflation, just as we ought to when looking in a mirror. It is a hard task. Getting beneath those projections is a journey in itself. The exercises in this book will help you explore your personal relationship with the cards so that ego and projection can take a backseat and allow truth to sit up front.

TOOLS FOR USING THIS BOOK

This book will be equal parts information and workbook. You will need a Tarot deck. I refer to the RWS deck in the exercises and Major and Minor Arcana descriptions because of its prominence and familiarity, but I do not view it as the only or the best deck available. Use a deck that you like. The best decks for self-readings have illustrated cards with characters or images that tell stories. Some decks, although absolutely lovely, do not provide enough pictorial fodder for storytelling. These can be more difficult to read, but they aren't impossible. If your deck does not speak to you in a way that you easily understand, consider trying a different deck. Later in the chapter I have included suggestions on how to select a good deck for self-reading.

Keep a journal or notebook handy for notes, thoughts, and revelations. My best students keep journals that are strictly for their Tarot work. I, however, have always been an anarchistic journaler, and my personal Tarot notes are scratched into books that also contain my personal thoughts, dreams, and shopping lists. Some students write their notes and interpretations directly onto their Tarot cards for easy access when doing their self-readings. There is nothing wrong with this in principle, and it certainly adds character to your deck. However, your relationship to the cards will evolve over time, and writing on the cards may stifle this process. Your associations will evolve. Notes on the cards can interrupt that. How you keep your notes is up to you, but keeping notes will be important, so don't skip this step.

Equally as important as your deck and journal is your sense of wonder. If you are already familiar with Tarot, bring along the interpretations you know, but do not cling to them. Give yourself the opportunity to see what secrets Tarot may have for you. If you are new to Tarot, take the interpretations in this book as inspiration, but don't resist your own should they differ from what you read. My interpretations are meant to unlock the door to

Tarot's mystique and help nudge you through it, as there may be a delicious surprise on the other side that is unique to you alone, but they are not meant to be final authority.

Should I Buy a Deck, or Should One Be Bought for Me?

I regularly hear a rumor that someone should never purchase their own Tarot deck and that it should only come as a gift. That is another fallacy. While there is certainly something special in being gifted a deck (several of my most beloved decks were gifts), a gifted deck is not automatically more powerful than one you purchase. Keep in mind that even decks produced by major publishing houses were likely designed by independent artists whose income relies on their royalties. Giving yourself permission to buy your own deck may help the production of other beautiful decks.

When I shop for decks, I look at the artwork. If it resonates with my taste and spirit, it's probably something I can use for readings. I have a friend who flips straight to the High Priestess card when considering a new deck. If he likes the depiction of the High Priestess, he likes the deck. Basically, if a deck calls to you, purchase it. Don't be afraid to purchase a particularly esoteric deck if you feel it's the right one. Also, don't be afraid to purchase a mainstream, commonly used deck if it speaks to you more than a fashionably obscure deck. Don't veer from second-hand decks. A deck does not need to be new to be yours. Often, previously owned decks have deep wisdom and a unique voice. I happen to love second-hand decks.

Whether your deck is new or previously loved, mass-produced or created by an independent artist, hold it in your hands. Does it feel alive? Do the images speak in a language that makes sense to you? Do you like its artwork? Does it feel familiar, even if it's new to you? If any of these questions are a yes, then you have found the right deck.

Using the Deck

Whether your deck is new or previously beloved, but especially if it is new, shuffle the cards. Some readers prefer a bridge riffle (as I do), and some are gentler with their cards. If your deck is old, rare, or fragile (many vintage or independently published decks come on thinner paper and are more easily damaged), it may be best to avoid riffle shuffling. Some readers place all of their cards facedown on a table and mix them all around. However you do it, it's best to shuffle before each reading.

Stop shuffling when the deck feels full. For some, this may mean there seems to be warmth or energy coming from the deck. Others count down in their head (7 . . . 6 . . . .5 . . . 4 . . .) before stopping. I personally shuffle until cards slip out of the deck. I also cut the deck when asking a question, splitting it randomly into two piles and dealing from the half of the deck not on top at the end of the shuffle.

Do I Need to Memorize All Seventy-Eight Cards?

No. In fact, I strongly encourage my students to avoid rote memorization. It *is* helpful to absorb a basic understanding of Tarot structure and the archetypal imagery, however. The age and complexity of the symbolic language will supply you with important information, but clinging to interpretations from a Tarot book is similar to memorizing vocabulary in a foreign language but never conversing with native speakers. Yes, you'll know the basic meanings of the words, but the nuances of spoken language will be lost. In short, you would be robbing yourself of a true conversation and the information that conversation might provide.

Over time, you will develop a unique language with Tarot. Your interpretations will likely bear similarities to what others see in Tarot, but there will always be blessed differences. In general, the Sun card means brightness and light. It does depict a sun, after all! The concept of the sun providing bright light is a universal image, as that is exactly what it does for the planet. However, one Tarot reader might see the Sun card as a positive omen— warmth, nurture, joy, and optimism. Another reader might see something less enticing: burns, unbearable heat, withered roots, a desert. Both interpretations are right, because both are rooted in the reader's experience. Knowing these personal interpretations seeds the ability to read one's own Tarot.

What If the Cards Come Out in Reverse?

If a card should appear reversed (upside down) and you are not familiar with reading reversed cards, my suggestion is to flip the card right side up for the first part of the book or until you are comfortable with them. We will do several exercises for understanding reversed cards. However, many excellent readers ignore reversed cards altogether. If you would rather not read reversals now or ever, I recommend infusing that intention into your deck while shuffling so the cards are aware you will be flipping them upright when dealt. I encourage you to try the reversal exercises when they arise, but know you don't ever have to read reversed cards if they never speak to you.

Caring for Your Cards

Like an instrument, decks develop their voice through use. The more you use a Tarot deck, the more accurate your readings will be. For practical reasons (such as keeping the cards clean and not losing them), keeping the deck in a bag is a good idea. Some believe keeping a deck in a silk bag will help the cards retain their power. If you like silk, you may like keeping your decks in a silk bag. However, maybe you like velvet. If so, consider storing your deck in a velvet bag. Maybe the fabric makes no difference to you. I personally don't believe one kind of fabric helps retain a deck's power more than another, but I do keep my decks in bags for the practical reasons above.

Some believe that no one but the reader should ever touch the reader's cards. I don't agree with this, either. When I read for others, I want them to cut the deck so the cards can respond to that querent's energy. I am fine then using that same deck for my self-readings. Then again, I have seen incredibly powerful readings by people who never allow others to touch their cards. I do see the merit of someone owning a Tarot deck for self-readings and being the only one to handle that particular deck, but it's not a practice I personally follow. Whether a person should handle your cards or not is entirely a matter of preference. But because of this, I do think it is very important to ask permission before touching another person's cards—every time. My husband reads Tarot, and even though I know he will always say yes, I still ask permission before handling his deck.

Will This Book Cover Other Types of Cards?

While many different types of cards make for excellent self-readings—oracle, Baraja, Lenormand, even standard playing cards—this book will focus on standard Tarot, a deck that has twenty-two Major Arcana and fifty-six Minor Arcana broken into four suits. If you practice another type of card divination, you will probably find some tools in here to enhance your readings, but other kinds of decks have their own unique systems of divining that I will not be able to cover in this book. Take what helps you, but if you are interested in a different kind of card system, it would be better to seek resources directly geared toward those decks.

Your Card of the Day

For the next week, <u>draw one card every morning.</u>

Do not try to divine the future based on the card. Simply get used to its images. Journal about your card. If you are unfamiliar with reversed cards (when the card comes out upside down), focus on the card in its upright position for a while. What is happening in the scene? What reactions do you have to the image? Is this card joyful or painful? How so? Does it remind you of a situation you are familiar with?

This morning, my card of the day was the Ace of Swords. I am drawn to the card's image of a hand holding a sword. The landscape looks barren, but the sword has a golden crown with leaves descending from it.

Victory?

My husband pulled the Ace of Wands. He pointed out the castle in the background and the rays coming off the hand holding the wand. There's a sense of <u>something flourishing</u> from this card, looking at the tiny leaves budding on it. He felt there was an <u>image of something sparking.</u>

Something coming forth

At the end of the day, journal about the day's events. What went right during your day? What went wrong? What were some general themes of your day (stress, happiness, fatigue, joy, surprises, mundane flow)? How do they relate to the image you saw on the card? What feelings were prevalent? You do not need to be familiar with the card to look for the parallels. Don't worry about whether you're "getting it right." This is an exercise of imagination and discovery, not testing your Tarot abilities.

After work, my husband and I compared our days in relation to the Tarot cards we'd pulled that morning. My day had been fraught with surprising challenges. It did feel a bit like I'd been sword fighting all day. At every turn there was some kind of stressful problem that needed the same focus I imagine a swordfight would require. For me, the Ace of Swords meant focus and staying alert in order to address problems as they happened.

My husband's day wasn't as challenging as mine, but it was unusually busy. The Ace of Wands, for him, spoke to the additional energy he felt he needed—like a zap to the day with a Magick wand—to keep up with the work. For him, the Ace of Wands meant personal power, sweat, and full attention to the work at hand.

For best results, try to put the card out of your mind during the day. Particularly if your card is one typically noted as a "scary card" (like the Tower or the Devil), it's possible to subconsciously create negative situations. Again, the goal is not to prophesize the future based on a card, but to learn the associations Tarot connects to your life and also for Tarot to learn your own associations with its imagery.

At the end of the week, reflect on the cards that came up for you. How do they match the blessings and challenges you encountered during the week? Were there any similarities between the cards? Any differences? Again, don't base your card interpretations on others' (say those you read in a book or on the Internet). Instead, draw parallels between the cards you pulled and the events you experienced. It is also okay to write down "I don't know." You are developing your own language and code with each card. Be adventurous and imaginative.

TWO

THE FOOL'S JOURNEY: THE STORY OF TAROT AND YOUR PLACE IN IT

You are the central character in your own personal myth. You have loved, lost, faced challenges, and challenged others. You've chosen paths and possibly wondered about those you didn't choose. You have felt joy and despair, weakness and strength, loneliness and community. You've been fueled by desires. You've tried to do right for yourself or others. This is true for me, for every reader of this book, and for everyone you know or have ever passed on the street. Our own stories may seem unique to us. If we reflect on our journeys as symbolic tapestries etched by our different stories, we will find individual threads in them that speak to us alone; but the overall picture will bear dramatic similarities to those representing the lives of our contemporaries, those who have gone before us, and those who have gone before them, stretching back to the beginning of humankind. These collected stories have shaped great myths and epic adventures. We then read them, hear them, watch them on screen. These familiar fictitious paths reflect our own journeys, allowing for deeper understanding of the significance of our own experiences. One of these stories is that of the Fool's journey, as reflected in the Major Arcana of the Tarot.

The twenty-two cards of the Major Arcana depict the great myths we personally lead. The word *myth* should not be taken as something false. Rather, myths are the poetic voice of common life experiences. As mentioned in chapter 1, it is this inclusion of the twenty-two Major Arcana cards that separates Tarot from other forms of playing cards. I have had students and clients not raised in the Western world (where the Major Arcana was born) find the Major Arcana often offers a direct parallel to mythic stories from their cultures.

The Major Arcana represents pivotal persons who have influenced us, as well as situations, lessons, conflicts, choices, and blessings that have shaped the course of our lives. Through their role in Tarot, the Major Arcana offers us the opportunity to reflect on these points and embrace them as the great mythic stories they truly are.

The card descriptions below reference the RWS deck. Some decks may have similar symbolism; others will be quite different. If your deck's images are different than the descriptions below and if it came with an accompanying book, you may want to reference it to better understand the artist's choice of symbolism. If your deck did not come with a book, make notes about what its images symbolize for you. Which stand out to you? What do the images remind you of? How might they connect with the descriptions you read below? How might they differ?

0: THE FOOL

The Main Character

When the Fool appears in readings I do for others, I often say, "Don't be offended, but this card is you." The main character in the Major Arcana is the Fool, marked by the number 0. This card might be better called the Seeker. In a deck I coproduced (Tarot of the Boroughs), we titled our 0 card the Seeker. While the Fool is often depicted as wide-eyed and possibly ignorant to danger (teetering dangerously close to a cliff's edge in most depictions), the Fool is not meant to be an idiot. The Fool is the set of eyes through which Tarot is viewed, and the primary recipient of its experiences.

Throughout this book, I use the gender pronouns most commonly associated with Tarot characters, but I do so with the understanding that each could easily materialize as any gender or devoid of gender altogether. However, because the Fool is the character through which we will view the entire Tarot for ourselves and must encompass the broadest experience, I use the gender-neutral term of they for broadest inclusion.

The Fool's Journey

While the Fool may be portrayed as naïve, they are not "foolish." They simply don't yet know what their journey holds for them. The Major Arcana celebrates that the Fool will be irrevocably changed at the end of their journey. Fools' journeys are often unintentional. Something happened to the Fool: there was a knock on their door, or "a funny thing happened on the way to someplace." In film and fiction, Fool characters can be found in Frodo in *The Lord of the Rings*, Luke Skywalker in *Star Wars: Episode IV—A New Hope*, or

Katniss in *The Hunger Games*. In each of these stories, the main characters were going about their business when an outside call, calamity, or other incident encouraged them to embark on extraordinary journeys. Through these journeys and through the characters they meet, they undergo massive transformations of the self.

We can view the Fool's journey as a single adventure or the story of an entire life. We come into this world knowing nothing and being wholly dependent on others, just as the Fool in the Major Arcana is wholly dependent on the first few characters they meet. In that context, the Major Arcana is a literal journey from birth to death. Through a microcosmic lens, we will each embody the Fool many times. Many students have found the Fool card to represent their experiences leaving a job or relationship and entering a new chapter in work or love. For some, it has meant a religious conversion. One person I knew felt the Fool represented the loss of his home by fire. While the loss was devastating, he found a strange freedom in being without material possessions. With the new opportunity to go anywhere he wanted, he took a chance and traveled the world.

When we imagine the Fool as ourselves, it profoundly enhances the significance of the other cards. Let us now become Fools and take a tour of the Major Arcana with the wide eyes and open heart indicated in that paramount card.

1. THE MAGICIAN

As traditionally imagined, the Magician is a stark contrast to the Fool. Whereas the Fool is wide-eyed and wandering, the Magician is grounded and solid, with all of his materials laid out in an organized fashion on a worktable. This is one of the, if not the first, characters the Fool meets. It is from the Magician that the Fool will learn the fundamental lessons they will draw upon for the rest of their journey. This is someone older, presumably wiser, and definitely more experienced than the Fool. The Magician recognizes the Fool's abilities and becomes their mentor, imparting the knowledge the Fool lacks.

In the first *Hunger Games* book, Haymitch Abernathy is the Magician to Katniss Everdeen's Fool. Haymitch is like Katniss in that he grew up in the same region as she, and he previously defeated the lethal game she is obligated to fight. Therefore, he mentors her in how to win the game. Like many Magician characters, Abernathy's direct time with Katniss is short. She is soon off on her own again, drawing from what tutelage she acquired, periodically receiving wisdom or assistance from him from afar. In many stories, this is the case with the Magician, whose memory stays with the Fool throughout the rest of their journey even though he may no longer be physically present.

For many of us, our Magicians are our primary mentors and teachers. The successful entrepreneur quoting their high school athletics coach is often considered cliché because it is such a common source of mentorship. Naturally, we rarely have just one person in the course of our lives who fills that role. Magicians appear whenever we are in need of direction, whether that be a dedicated elementary school teacher or a stranger providing directions when we arrive in a new city.

2. THE HIGH PRIESTESS

The High Priestess (sometimes called the Popess in older decks) is a character of esoteric wisdom who awakens the Fool to the spiritual aspect of their journey. She is crowned by the moon, a lunar crescent at her feet. Her throne is positioned between two pillars, one black and the other white. She may appear as an unusual character in the world of the Fool, or she may represent a profound vision. However she manifests, the High Priestess draws an element of the supernatural into the Fool's world. The deeper implications of the journey become clearer.

In *The Lord of the Rings*, this character could be envisioned as Galadriel, the Elf Queen who provides Frodo and his Fellowship with not only tests of their resolve but also Magickal cloaks and supplies that will aid them throughout their quest. She reveals to Frodo the serious, overarching nature of his journey as well as the unseen forces supporting it. She is evocative of the moment when spiritual forces meet practical experiences.

While the High Priestess could be a personal guru, she could also represent a mystical experience that shapes the work we do going forward. For me, a High Priestess moment was, as a teenager, walking into a New Age store in my hometown and receiving my first professional Tarot reading. The new, deeply mystical experience illuminated a new view of Spirit, outside of the Church and parochial school I'd always known. Although I've had hundreds of readings since, the mystique and Magick of that first reading has forever touched not only the way I do my own readings but also the way I view their spiritual implications.

3. THE EMPRESS

The Empress, decked in jewels, surrounded in comfort, and often depicted as pregnant, is the card of the Mother. In the Fool's journey, this is when the Fool knows their mother. It may be the moment when the Fool meets their mother for the very first time. It may also be when the Fool knows their mother as a person, perhaps one with needs herself and not simply as the one who provides. Perhaps this is the moment when the Fool leaves their mother behind to go on their journey. It might be when the Fool becomes a mother themselves.

In *Back to the Future*, Marty McFly travels back in time in his Fool's journey, and his Empress moment appears when one of the first people he meets in his journey is his mother as a teenager. For the first time, he learns about her outside of the role of "Mom," and through that, he gains deeper insight into the nature of his whole family. In *The Color Purple*, Celie encounters the Empress when she becomes her—both when she gives birth and when she becomes stepmother to her husband's children.

Our Empress moments vary. While I doubt anyone will go back in time, an Empress moment might be learning about a maternal figure's past, helping us better understand her as a person. If someone was adopted, maybe an Empress moment is meeting their birth mother. Like Celie, our Empress encounters might be when we become mothers or take on maternal roles. We may also encounter the Empress when we create—be it a business, an organizing endeavor, an art or writing project, or something else altogether. One friend of mine had an Empress moment when she began rescuing and fostering laboratory rats!

For me, an Empress moment happened when I was six years old. Our family was in the process of moving from Tennessee to Oregon. My sister and I found our mother crying in the kitchen. She explained she was sad to leave her friends behind, even though the move would be good for our family. I remember being stunned. My little girl mind had not imagined that Mommy might have feelings about the move. Before that moment, Mommy was who took care of my sister and me. Suddenly, Mommy was a person.

The Empress marks the point in our Fool's journey when we come to know truths about the role of the mother, whether these be blessed or painful truths. They may also be moments when we know the Empress through becoming her, through our giving birth to people or projects, or becoming caretakers of persons or things outside ourselves. When we experience the Empress, our journey is no longer only about us. Part of who we are, and therefore our journey, is deeply influenced by how we affect others.

4. THE EMPEROR

In Tarot, the counterpart to the maternal Empress is the paternal Emperor. He sits on a stone throne, a golden crown on his head. Beneath his robe, he appears to wear armor. The Emperor and the Empress represent the Fool's parents or parental figures. As in the meeting of the Empress, the Fool meets, knows, or understands their father. The Emperor, like the Empress, is a beacon of love for the Fool, but because Tarot stems from a more patriarchal time and place in history, the Emperor has traditionally inherited more of a sense of structure than the more nurturing influences traditionally assigned to the Empress. This structure is one that often represents personal or family ethics and ideology, as opposed to societal structure (which we'll see more of in the next card, the Hierophant). The Emperor is also traditionally a card of wisdom.

One of the best-known examples of the Fool meeting the Emperor comes from Shakespeare's *Hamlet*, in which the young prince Hamlet encounters the ghost of his murdered father. In this encounter, the ghost explains the circumstances around his death. In this example, the Emperor moment is the actual "knock on the door" that starts Hamlet on his Fool's journey for revenge and redemption. In another example, the film *Forrest Gump* includes an Emperor moment at the end of the journey when the main character, Forrest, discovers he has fathered a child.

Emperor moments may be similar to those of the Empress. Perhaps we become fathers or paternal figures. It may mean meeting a biological father we never knew. My own father likes to quote a Mark Twain story in which the teenaged Twain couldn't tolerate the enormity of his father's ignorance. The twenty-one-year-old Twain is shocked by how much his father learned in just a few short years. In that anecdote, Twain's own maturity and clarity about his father's wisdom is a Fool's journey Emperor moment.

Emperor moments may mean shattered visions of who we believed our fathers to be. Some of my students have talked about their Emperor moments through meeting estranged fathers. One of my students described his Emperor moment as learning his absent father wasn't the hero he believed him to be. Another said her Emperor moment was reuniting with her estranged father and learning he was a sad, lonely person and not the wicked character she remembered. Emperor moments may mean stepping into the role of fatherhood or co-parenting. Also, as with the Empress, an Emperor moment may be assuming a position of responsibility, such as in a company or a cause. The difference between Empress and Emperor moments with regards to responsibilities comes from the inception of those responsibilities. Empress moments generally occur when we create something ourselves, such as starting a business. A comparable Emperor moment might be supporting a start-up or inheriting an already established business.

5. THE HIEROPHANT

The Hierophant also sits on a throne, but he wears religious vestments. This is the Fool's primary encounter with authority outside of their home. When Tarot was first produced, the Church had primary authority, sometimes even rivaling the ruling queen or king. The original Hierophant card was called the Pope. This card might have marked the Catholic rite of Confirmation, in which a young person is presented to the Church community as an adult. The Hierophant card represents understanding structure and authority, via the wisdom of navigating a system. If the Magician showed the Fool how to drive and the High Priestess provided the map, the Hierophant now instructs the Fool on the rules of the road.

When Harry Potter arrived at Hogwarts School of Witchcraft and Wizardry, Professors McGonagall and Dumbledore embody the Hierophant role through explaining the rules of the school to the incoming students—both the expectations of the school and the forbidden areas, as well as facilitating their residential house selection. A more sinister Hierophant can be seen in *The Shawshank Redemption*'s Warden Samuel Norton, who set and explained the rules of the prison to the incoming inmates, but who also used both religion and systematic discipline to manipulate the system for his own gain. In both stories, the central characters are introduced to the structure and rules of new institutions and authority via these embodiments of the Hierophant.

In the contemporary world, experience with the Hierophant might be college orientation or military boot camp. I sometimes cite the Hierophant as the human resources manager who explains the company policies to a new hire, and for a time becomes the living embodiment of that company's structure and order. However, because the Hierophant does have religious connotations, other Hierophant moments might also be the Bat or Bar Mitzvah, baptism or Confirmation, or a conversion to a new religion.

6. THE LOVERS

The sixth card in the Major Arcana illustrates the Fool's first consensual experience with intimacy and love. The earliest Tarot cards depict a blindfolded Cupid aiming an arrow at an unsuspecting couple, marking the surprising partnerships and timing of such entanglements. Yet the Lovers represents more than interpersonal chemistry. In the Fool's journey, it symbolizes a kind of love that changes the heart of the Fool. They cannot go back to the character they were before they encountered the Lovers. It marks connections so deeply profound that they change who we are, where we go, and how we see the world.

In *Fiddler on the Roof*, the young character Hodel is strictly adherent to her traditional faith and upbringing at the beginning of the story, yet she finds her worldview twisted when she falls in love with the radical Perchik. As she leaves her beloved home to follow him to a strange city, she says to her father, Tevye, "Who could see that a man would come who would change the shape of my dreams?" Love, changing the course of the Fool's journey, is a trademark of the Lovers card.

The Lovers card can mark for us a first love, or a sexual or intimate encounter. For some, it might be losing their virginity. For others, it might be awakening to sexual preference. It might also be meeting a life mate. Finally, a Lovers moment might not be a person, but a passion. One Lovers card story I heard took the form of an ailing feline. A career-focused woman heard the cat crying from a sewer ditch, and although she was dressed for an important meeting, she climbed into wet filth to rescue her. She blew off the meeting to spend a day at the vet. The cat did not survive, but the woman stayed with the cat until the end, ensuring the little animal was comfortable and at peace. In that experience she found her true love was animal rescue, and she left a successful career as an investment banker to start an animal shelter. Meeting her Lovers card in the form of a sick cat was the start of her own Fool's journey.

As you can probably tell by now, the Major Arcana is a prototype for a journey, but when the Fool's journey manifests in our lives, it rarely makes the kind of orderly sense that the Major Arcana would have us believe. In addition, these cards will not always portend the life-shaking implications as mentioned above. Receiving the Lovers in a reading does not automatically mean you are immediately bound for a life-changing sort of love. Maybe it will encourage increased quality time with someone or something you love. Maybe it will remind you of a previous Lovers card moment. One of Tarot's greatest gifts is its way of anchoring us to our true selves when life starts to veer us off-course. Through the Lovers card, it says, "Remember what you love."

7. THE CHARIOT

Until this point in the Fool's journey, other people have directly influenced the Fool's experiences. Parents, mentors, institutions, and even lovers initially shape the course of the Fool's life; but via the Chariot card the Fool is completely in control of themselves. In the RWS deck, this card is depicted as a charioteer driving two sphinxes of opposing colors. In some decks, the creatures rear in opposite directions, indicating the sometimes messy path personal journeys can take. Ultimately, the Chariot represents the Fool's first taste of self-direction, personal accountability, and, most of all, freedom. This image of controlling the unwieldy is also a symbol of the Fool learning to control their internal impulses, emotions, and words.

In *Star Wars: Episode IV—A New Hope*, the Chariot is represented by the Millennium Falcon, which first provided enterprise to the smuggler Han Solo and later escape, before finally becoming a vessel of power to the rest of the rebellion. When the characters first encounter the Millennium Falcon they are nervous about its seemingly rickety appearance, but the aircraft still manages to transport them to the next stage of their journey. While aboard the Falcon, the characters learn how to live and work together, taming their personal impulses and tempers in order to be a stronger unit.

The Chariot may be defined by getting a driver's license or a passport. It might also be graduation from college or trade school, moving into a first apartment or home, or leaving one career to start another one. It is a point of departure where we are free to carve out our own rules and create our own institutions, along with the "wild card" moments that come along with that.

My personal Chariot moment was my move to New York. I had just finished college and started a life for myself three thousand miles away from my hometown. I was no longer defined by rules of upbringing, institution, and being the person others knew me to be. In college, I started exploring Wicca and wanted to get deeper into it, but my college was only a few miles from where I'd grown up and where I was known as "Catholic Courtney." Talking about my new faith yielded snickers and comments such as "Sure you are, *Catholic Courtney*!" It can be hard to grow into a new sense of self when everyone around you "knew you when"! Moving to a place where I knew no one allowed me to stretch and explore my faith and other things about me, but this was also a time when I needed to shape my previously do-whatever-whenever/dress-however college lifestyle into one that fit a Monday through Friday, nine-to-five lifestyle. In addition, the culture of the new city required a different sort of conforming. Leaving my ID at home and apologizing profusely to the bouncer might have worked at a club in my hometown. It did not work in NYC. Sitting on the fire escape on a sunny day might be an acceptable norm at my old home. It could get me fined or arrested in my new home. Yes, there was freedom, but there was also a need to tame a few impulses for the sake of moving forward in my life.

8. STRENGTH

In Strength, the Fool's resolve is tested. The Strength card is traditionally depicted as a woman, crowned with the symbol for infinity, calmly placing a hand into an angry lion's mouth. It's a strange-sounding image, but one defined as the Fool drawing from the wisdom of both their primary teachings and their own intuitive impulses in facing a seemingly impossible challenge. They are forced to face something. Maybe they want to overcome fear. Maybe they have no other alternative. Either way, they must pass through the obstacle to complete the journey.

Near the end of the television series *Breaking Bad*, Jesse Pinkman is locked in an underground cell and forced to produce drugs daily while chained. One night, he breaks out of his cell by standing on tiptoe on the bucket he uses as a toilet, stretching and straining to maneuver the lock open with his fingertips, and pulling himself up with weakened, overworked arms. This scene is one of the most poignant Strength card moments I've seen on modern television. So much of the character's power had been taken away, but he dug to the deepest part of himself to pull out the remaining strength he had in an attempt to gain his freedom.

A Strength moment in my own journey wasn't nearly as dire (thankfully) as the *Breaking Bad* example. I was a volunteer chaplain in the Occupy Wall Street movement. I sat in the medical tent in Zuccotti Park and listened to people who needed an ear. One day, a man who was having a psychotic break interrupted the General Assembly to proclaim himself not only the leader of the intentionally leaderless movement but also the Messiah. My Strength moment came in the form of gentleness, coaxing the man to come out of the working group he was disrupting to pray with me on the street corner. It took focus, patience, and stillness on my part, which aren't attributes I come by naturally. But in the moment, I found strength—not only to keep the man from disrupting the work of others, but also to coax his cell phone from him to call his wife and let her know he needed more help than the team at the Occupy medical tent could provide.

Strength appears in our journeys when praxis becomes practical. We may believe we know certain things about ourselves, but only in Strength card moments do we know the depth of our resolve. We may believe we fear fire but discover we are calm and collected if we actually need to escape from a burning building. These Strength moments may require brute force or they may be seemingly simple moments, such as holding our tongues when it's imperative that we do so. Strength stretches our boundaries and shows us our greatest potential.

9. THE HERMIT

THE HERMIT.

The Fool meets the Hermit when they are lost or exhausted with their journey. The Hermit is often shown as a frail, elderly man carrying a lantern. This lantern lights the way for the Fool. The Hermit often appears unexpectedly and provides a source of strength, wisdom, and sometimes healing. Although the Hermit lives apart from the mainstream world, he may be familiar with the Fool's journey. In general, the Hermit appears when the Fool is in a time of need, but he does not attend to them for long. Some interpretations say the Hermit is the Fool in midlife.

In the novel *Beloved*, pregnant Sethe flees enslavement by running through the forest. When she is so weakened by her journey that she cannot run any more, she meets Amy Denver, who has just completed indentured servitude. In a deserted and secluded building, Amy delivers the baby and nurses Sethe back to health. While their journeys are different, there is a mutual understanding of where each of them has come from and what they have experienced. When Sethe's health returns, the two women continue on their respective paths.

In our journeys, the Hermit appears when we believe we cannot go on alone or when we may have lost our way. Medical persons, particularly in the ICU or rehabilitative centers, serve as the Hermit, healing broken parts of ourselves in a setting outside of our normal lives. A casual, or meaning-ful, conversation with a stranger in passing can also be a Hermit moment. My husband and I had a powerful Hermit moment one evening after a bad interaction with a cab driver. The driver was angry, hostile, and frankly, scared us. When he finally let us out, we were still far from home and hailed another cab. Our next driver was calm and kind. When we told him what had happened with our first driver, he thoughtfully referenced beliefs from his Islamic faith and his own experiences as an NYC taxi driver, helping us view our previous driver with a little more compassion, while also finding compassion for ourselves. The Hermit not only shows us a view of our paths from a different angle, but also reminds us of beauty and grace when the world has grown mean.

10. WHEEL OF FORTUNE

WHEEL of FORTUNE.

Strengthened by their time with the Hermit, the Fool begins their journey again through the Wheel of Fortune. Traditional Wheel of Fortune cards show a disk inscribed with several languages, surrounded by archangels and deities from ancient Egypt. While there are great spiritual forces at play, a wheel does not turn without earthly impetus. The Fool's luck is changed in the Wheel of Fortune because the Fool causes it to move. The point in the journey may feel like a blessing, but it's not one that simply happens. The blessing occurs because the Fool changes their own luck.

Unlike the previous Tarot characters, the Wheel of Fortune does not just appear. The Wheel of Fortune represents an internal choice on our part to continue when it would be easier to give up. A friend of mine experienced the Wheel of Fortune after he was attacked while heading home from a night shift at his job. When he recovered from his injuries (resting in privacy, like the Hermit card part of his journey), he left his job, where he hadn't been happy in the first place, and enrolled in school to pursue a different career. He deliberately changed the course of his own fate. There was considerable work involved but a substantial reward: two trademarks of the Wheel of Fortune.

The Wheel can also represent industry. As Tarot was first constructed from paper products which required the work of a water wheel, this card can mean invention. In the realm of our journeys, these inventions are meant to dramatically improve our lives. It may mean an actual physical invention, or it can be a new health or fitness routine. It may also mean that we fully embrace authority over our own actions. A friend of mine used to say, "I'm turning my wheel!" whenever she was working to improve something in herself or heal from an emotional injury that was holding her back.

The commonality among different Wheel of Fortune moments is that they are rooted in personal agency. The Wheel embodies not just changes to ourselves but also the changes we choose to make.

11. JUSTICE

At this point in the journey, the Fool is faced with consequence. The card of Justice, represented by a seated judge holding a sword and a set of scales, determines what the Fool owes versus what the Fool is owed. Enemies from the past may return. Likewise, good deeds may be repaid. The card represents a restoration of balance. Any imbalances the Fool created or received so far in the journey will be rectified—whether the Fool likes it or not.

In *Willy Wonka and the Chocolate Factory,* Mr. Wonka set up Mr. Slugworth to test the honesty and resolve of the children visiting his factory. When the central character Charlie Bucket proved his loyalty and integrity, Mr. Wonka rewarded him with ownership of the factory and all of his "candy-making secrets."

A real-life example of justice can be found in the memoir and later television series *Orange Is the New Black*, in which the central character of Piper is arrested for a crime she committed ten years prior. Although she had moved on from her past to live a quiet, law-abiding life, the past eventually demanded that she repay her debt to society.

Justice card moments may be scary or disruptive, such as when a loan may suddenly come due. They may also be blessed, such as taking a vacation with hard-saved money. Another example might be having good health in our later years as a result of eating healthy food and exercising regularly in our youth. Another version of Justice might be receiving accolades for a job well done or a thank-you note for a kindness or gift.

The Justice card may appear for us as lessons yet to be learned or work undone. It may not necessarily be "punishment" or "reward." It might be the resolution of an old rift. It might be the completion of a promise you made to yourself or others. Many of my clients and students ask about closure with regards to romantic or platonic relationships gone wrong. Justice may signify the closure craved, or it may symbolize acceptance that some answers will never be found.

The Justice card reminds us of the imprints we make on ourselves and this world of ours, and how we bless and injure both. Nothing in this world happens in a vacuum. Every action we take creates a ripple that eventually finds its way back to us, for better or for worse. It also reminds us that we can't always walk away from unfinished business. Sooner or later, we may need to complete what we thought was behind us.

12. THE HANGED MAN

Despite good intentions and internalizing wisdom learned from others or from experiences, there comes a time when the Fool gets stuck. Unlike the Hermit or the first few characters of the Major Arcana, the Hanged Man is less a person the Fool comes across and more one they become for a period of time. The Fool is suspended upside down by one leg on a gallows. Every other moment in the Fool's journey involves choice. But in the Hanged Man, there are no other options than surrender. The Fool is forced to give themselves over to the circumstances and possibly surrender all they have worked for. The journey seems hopeless, and the goal seems out of reach.

A commonly known image of the Hanged Man would be Jesus Christ suspended on the cross. After a tumultuous journey packed with fame as well as persecution and resistance, Jesus was captured by his government and suspended on two crossbeams. There was no escape, no possible movement. His only choice was to "give up the ghost" and surrender his last breath. The following two cards, Death and then Temperance, are strongly linked to this biblical story. Connecting the Hanged Man to the loss embodied in Death and the rest in the tomb implied in Temperance help us best understand the Hanged Man.

While some may argue that Jesus on the cross is an example of martyrdom, the Hanged Man manifests as sacrifice, but not specifically martyrdom. A martyr chooses to make a sacrifice of themselves, but the Hanged Man usually represents a sacrifice when there is no other alternative. The employer who is faced with a decision to either make layoffs or lose the business is facing the Hanged Man. Likewise, the person who is unable to pay a mortgage faces the choice of selling the house or having it be repossessed by the bank is another Hanged Man battle. Whatever the case may be, the Hanged Man represents difficult decisions, often one in which the circumstances have all but made the decision for the person.

The Hanged Man represents sacrifice as the only choice. It involves the humility of accepting that we are powerless within a specific situation. But as in the story of Christ on the cross, the Hanged Man does not represent finality, but the moment before a massive transition.

13. DEATH

Death immediately follows the Hanged Man. The classic image of the Death card shows a skeletal figure trampling the paths of peasants and kings alike, symbolizing that no one is immune to death. Yet, it is not the Fool's physical death. The journey is far from complete. The story of the Major Arcana connects Death and the Hanged Man for good reason. In order to move forward, the Fool must sacrifice. At this point, the Fool experiences loss—of freedom, choice, or companionship. Something in the Fool's life, or perhaps something within the Fool themselves, has to symbolically or actually die in order for the journey to continue.

Listing a single Death incident from a film or book is a tough call. Loss is natural to all journeys—lives, relationships, money, property, and more. Sometimes it's natural to the story. Other times, it seems to be simply a cruel trick of the Universe. My generation may remember the scene in the film version of *The NeverEnding Story* when the main character Atreyu lost his horse Artax in the swamp during his journey. The loss was devastating to Atreyu (as well as to everyone born in the late '70s and early '80s) and changed the shape of the rest of his journey. Yet Atreyu had a choice in Artax's loss. He could have let it throw him off his path. He could have chosen to follow his beloved horse into the swamp. Yet he chose to keep going. One message of the Death card is that while it marks a loss in our journey, it does not mark the end of us.

Of all the cards in the Major Arcana, the Death card is the only one each of us is sure to experience. Fortunately, Death card moments aren't automatically deaths of those we love. They can mark any significant loss.

After the 2008 economic crash, my Tarot clients frequently received the Death card, marking the significant job losses many of them experienced. The promise in those moments is that there was an opportunity to do something different, perhaps to do something they loved even more. It was a chance for transformation. Death card moments can also represent major shifts in the way we live. Sometimes, this can be a positive thing. A good friend of mine received the Death card in a reading they did for themselves just prior to becoming engaged. Rather than an ominous sign, the card symbolized the "death" of a solitary life and the merging into life with another person (and they remain happily married to this day!).

The Death card does mark an ending. It's often a jarring or painful one, but not always. Sometimes it can include a blessed beginning. One of the greater truths to the Death card is that it is natural. As it's said in the fantasy fiction series A Song of Ice and Fire and in the subsequent television show Game of Thrones, Valar morghulis, which means "All men must die." So must all endeavors, ambitions, and even relationships to the passage of time or physical death. But in all of these situations, it can be argued that nothing is ever truly lost—everything simply transforms. This is a truth of the Death card.

14. TEMPERANCE

Temperance is the Fool's lesson in balance. Because of where it resides in Tarot (after the Hanged Man and Death), it also can mean a kind of resurrection. After the losses via the Hanged Man and Death, the Fool is living with a new simplicity, perhaps preparing to rebuild after having lost so much. Above all, the Fool must focus on lessons learned and develop moderation and patience. The deepest lessons from the Temperance card may come when reflecting on it in relation to Hanged Man and/or Death card experiences. Yet we do not have to experience both of the prior cards to experience Temperance. Nor do we need to experience them sequentially. However it manifests, Temperance represents a second chance—one that is accompanied by compromise and creating equilibrium.

Several years ago, a friend of mine wasn't feeling very well and went to the doctor. The doctor determined my friend was suffering a life-threatening illness that required a lifestyle change. I personally see the Death card as letting go of a lifestyle that was killing him. Temperance is the life of compromise he needed to lead after such a close call with death, a compromise that included new ways to eat, drink, and care for his personal health.

Circumstances need not always be extreme to experience Temperance. Temperance may come when we hit proverbial brick walls, lose our patience, or exhaust ourselves. Some Temperance card moments might include working out a compromise with a partner or friend after a particularly trying time in the relationship. Temperance appears after something tells us to stop, to look at what is happening to us, and listen to what changes we need to make. Temperance cleans up personal aftermath in a systematic fashion. We rebalance ourselves so that we do not undergo the same lesson. But, as any yoga practitioner will attest, balance is both experience and choice. Our Temperance moments do not sprout from vacuums but through moments in time that give us pause, nudging us into commitment with equilibrium.

15. THE DEVIL

At this stage of the journey, the Fool may believe that the worst is behind them, but they still need to meet their nemesis. Dorothy faces the Wicked Witch of the West. The prince fights the dragon outside Sleeping Beauty's castle. Frodo walks into Mordor. In many of these stories, this is the apex of the Fool's journey, but it isn't the final challenge. Dorothy and Frodo still have to get home, and Sleeping Beauty still needs to be awoken. These Devils are shadows of the protagonists on their journeys. They represent all that the characters fear and despise, and things that keep them from their goals. The Devil is frequently the trickiest or even the most painful card the Fool will experience, but it is often the greatest learning experience as well.

The aforementioned are simple Devils. The Devil is a single character whom the Fool must face, one they receive a great deal of assistance in fighting. Once the Devil is felled, the danger has passed and the Fool is free to return to normal life. Devils are far more complicated in real life. They might appear as a single person, but they are equally as likely to show up as a system or situation. Their defeat will probably not come in a single battle and might need be navigated, distracted, or negotiated.

The film *Hotel Rwanda* details the true story in which hotel owner Paul Rusesabagina housed and protected nearly fifteen hundred people during the Rwandan genocide. In this example, the Devil appears in several guises:

the extremism that fueled the killing campaign, the foreknowledge but unwillingness of other world powers to prevent the situation and their lack of action when it began, and, if going back further in time, the colonialism that divided the people and set them against one another. This story of Rusesa-bagina wasn't solved in one fight, but through a series of negotiations, bribes, and other cunning acts against the various groups threatening his guests.

Devils are constant in our journeys. They may be competitors or ene-mies. They may be racist, classist, sexist, phobic, or other systems that inflict violence against us. Other Devils are internal. They can surface as eating disorders, addictions, or other emotional, mental, or physical illnesses. They may be aspects of character that harm the self or others. They may even be our self-doubts or fears. In other journeys, the Devil may pop up ran-domly as an obstacle on the path. No matter their identity, a Devil must be defeated, or at least placated, if we are to persevere and complete the journey we've started.

16. THE TOWER

The next card in this series of "Rough Lessons" in the Major Arcana is the Tower, in which the Fool experiences a great upheaval from an outside force. The card is often repre-sented by lightning striking a stone tower. Rubble tumbles from the structure. Symbolically, an existing structure in the Fool's life, previously thought unshakable, is razed. Whether human-made or an act of the gods (or a combination thereof), the Fool's journey will not be the same.

Years ago, I dreamed I stood on the top floor of a sky-scraper. It twisted and collapsed, but I walked out of the rub-ble unharmed. Later that week, my company laid off a person I believed was critical to the institution. The loss impacted the entire staff and board, and it was certainly a period of upheaval. While I was sorry to see this person go, I took on a few of their duties (a way of picking up the rubble), and by doing so, my own job security increased.

I have seen the Tower suggest a move to a more prosperous area, a pregnancy or birth, or an unexpected romance that "turns a person's world upside down. I've also seen it mean a great loss, such as a sudden death or a fire. The attack on the World Trade Center on September 11, 2001, included two literal fallen towers. The grave upheaval of personal loss, sense of safety, and reorganization of national security was felt worldwide. Truly, the world was not the same after that Tower moment in our collective Fool's journey. But as I write this, the new Freedom Tower, the tallest building in the Western Hemisphere, is now open on the same place where the Twin Towers stood, marking the period of renewal.

Many moments can be illustrated by several different Tarot cards. Tower moments can even feel like Death card moments because of the losses they often carry. For example, those who remember the September 11th attacks may likely associate the event with Death for its loss, the Devil for its design as an enemy attack, and possibly the Emperor for its political connotations. I also associate the Temperance card with 9/11 for the increased security procedures we now live with because of the attack. These are all true, but what is significant about 9/11 being a particular embodiment of the Tower is that it was the collapse of a structure created by people and believed to be permanent. When the Tower falls, it almost always takes those it affects by complete surprise.

The upheaval moments in the Tower can certainly be traumatic, but not all of them will be. Many can also be enlightening. When I've suffered from frustrating writer's block, the moment it finally gives way is a blessed Tower moment, as the block is usually one I've unwittingly self-created and in difficult moments imagine to be permanent. One Tarot reader friend of mine calls the Tower the "aha" moment, in which beliefs and structures previously and fervently clung to give way in the name of progress and enlightenment.

Ultimately, the greatest blessing in the Tower card is the opportunity to rebuild.

17. THE STAR

At this point, the Fool has survived the most difficult parts of the journey and has every reason to give up. But in the Star card, the clouds part and light makes its way to the Fool's path. They remember their initial calling. They keep going, fueled by only hope, as hope may be the one thing that has not been taken from them. We can consider the Star card the North Star of a navigational path. The Fool is back in touch with that which guides them. However, most of the characters that helped shape the Fool's calling are no longer with them. They are alone at this point in their journey, but the voices of the past urge them forward, and the promise of completion and attainment still beckons.

In my journey as an activist, Star card moments have been integral to my continuing the work when it truly felt hopeless. Whether that battle was opposing a war, fighting for an historic church, or opposing hydraulic fracturing, each was its own Fool's journey and each had a moment (often, several such moments) when the outlook was bleak and quitting was appealing. During those moments, it felt as though there were plenty of other things I could have been doing with my time, things that wouldn't feel like I was waving signs on the deck of a sinking ship. Yet each of those battles found me alone at some point, quite often staring at the stars, and deciding to continue the fight even if it meant the end product would only be picking up rubble. While I still can't celebrate the end of my country's wars, I have been able to celebrate the successful restoration of a gorgeous cathedral, the abolition of hydraulic fracturing in New York State, and marriage equality in my nation.

The Star card reminds us that even when times are quite dark, hope is not lost. It also reminds us that many things can be taken away from us through fate, time, and circumstance, but only hope can be surrendered voluntarily. The trick of the Star card is that it is often not an omen of a specific event. It frequently indicates a moment of choice. We choose to have hope. We choose to place faith. We choose to keep going toward something uncertain even when every logical sign says to stop.

18. THE MOON

The Fool is still traveling through a darker part of the journey, but the path is now better illuminated. The Moon sheds light on confusing things, giving them shape and context. Mysteries are solved, at least partially. Memories may drift to the surface. With the light of the Moon, the Fool is better equipped to navigate the remainder of their journey.

However, the Moon has not always had a positive connotation in Tarot. Earlier decks and writings associated the Moon with "lunacy," or the Fool losing their grip on reality. Rachel Pollack points out in her book, *Tarot Wisdom*, that the columns of the High Priestess card, the sphinxes of the Chariot, and the chained demons of the Devil all have stark black-and-white divisions, but in the Moon card the pillars in the background are a soft gray.[1] This seems to suggest that the Fool's perceptions of power, place, prominence, and everything else have shifted. Whether or not the Fool is actually suffering from a mental breakdown is undetermined. The Fool may simply feel like they are "going crazy" as the world they thought they knew no longer looks like the one they live in. But the message of the Moon is not to question the Fool's perception of reality, but rather to show that it has shifted. Perhaps the trials of the Tower, Death, or otherwise have radically altered life so much that they cannot go back to the world they once knew. At the very least, they cannot look at it in the same way.

I met a man who struggled personally, socially, and professionally for years. He felt he was different than other people but couldn't articulate how. Because of this lack of specificity, he couldn't find any tools to bridge the gaps that set him back in so many areas of his life, including personal relationships and professional successes. When he was finally diagnosed with a specific cognitive delay, things finally made logical sense. The struggles he previously experienced didn't evaporate, but the new information helped him better navigate them. A great mystery in his life was solved. His world itself had not changed, but how he viewed it certainly did. He had more light, like that of the full moon on a dark night, to better see his journey.

The Moon card might be experienced through the revelation of a family secret, or through a personal revelation that redefines a person's life, such as accepting sexual orientation, gender identity, or a religious belief that differs from what they were taught growing up. It may be information that changes the way we look at things: "I'll never eat sausage again now that I've seen how it's made."

The Moon doesn't remove obstacles, but its light helps us understand and maneuver them. One of the beautiful truths of the Moon card is in the different animals gazing up at it—the crawfish and the wolves. No matter the species, all of us have experienced the Moon. All of us, at some point, will have a truth revealed to us—whether blessed or painful—that will permanently alter the way we see things. Finally, the actual Moon's shift through different phases over the course of a month remind us that when we receive the Moon card in a reading, feelings of disorientation that might accompany the stark revelations are phases in themselves. In time, we will settle into the new world illuminated so very differently by our Moon card moments.

19. THE SUN

The Sun card frequently shows a baby riding on the back of a pony, the golden sun shining onto the child. It is a picture of pure joy. It carries the symbol of starting over, as do many images in the Major Arcana. However, this "fresh start" for the Fool is different from the other cards in that the Fool's circumstances may not have changed, but their perspective has shifted. Perhaps this is in finally being comfortable with the new worldview the Fool found in the Moon. Perhaps this is a new aura of confidence that doesn't come from the approval of others, but from the self. However this new viewpoint may manifest, the Fool has re-embraced their journey with a tenacity matched only by a child. Some deep thinkers say the second half of one's life involves tearing down walls that one spent the first half of one's life building. In the Sun card, those walls are far behind the Fool. They have nothing to hold them back and everything to gain.

Robert V. O'Neill says in *Tarot Symbolism* that the Sun card is the vision of the Fool walking out of Plato's cave: "He no longer sees reality as shadows on the cave wall. Now he sees the sun in direct, full glory. The barren landscape of the Moon has turned into sunlight, grass, and flowers. The Fool has reached the summit of the natural life. This is as far as he can go on his own power."[2]

The final scene in the first *Rocky* film is one I view as the Sun card in action. Rocky faces a supposedly unbeatable opponent in the boxing ring.

Rocky turns out to not be a match for his opponent in skill and experience, but his tenacity is unequaled. While he ultimately does not win the fight, his zeal, exuberance, and complete lack of inhibition grant him success in his personal goal, which was simply to "go the distance." Just as O'Neill mentioned, Rocky went as far as he could go on his own power.

The personal power represented by the Sun is not that which is reflected in accomplishments or the opinions of others. It is a moment of complete confidence in ourselves, because we are ourselves. Maybe these are moments in which we are like Rocky. Maybe it seems the world thinks we are crazy, but for a moment, we don't care. I once saw a YouTube video of a middle-aged, obese woman in sweatpants dancing in a shopping mall. She was completely enthralled with the music. People stared, some snickered. While many of the video's comments were kind and loving, some were not. This woman was probably not ignorant to the stares or the verbal bullying, but the jubilation in her steps suggested she did not care. She was the embodiment of the Sun in the Fool's journey. Whether she had just received the greatest news of her life or simply loved the song on the loudspeaker, it didn't matter. She was experiencing pure abandon of restriction and criticism and embracing the joy of the Sun card. It showed in her steps.

20. JUDGMENT

The Judgment card often shows an angel parting the clouds above and blaring a trumpet at Earth. The Dead awaken from their graves, perhaps to ascend to the heavens. For the Fool, it means receiving a call from Spirit as they approach the end of their journey. This may be in the form of an invitation to another journey or a call of clarity to know what their journey has been about this entire time. Waite described the card as one that acknowledges the great transformation the Fool has undergone, and it embraces the joy or perhaps fear that comes along with that acknowledgment.[3] Maybe this recognition comes to the Fool from an outside source (think of the awards the Wizard gives to Dorothy's companions at the end of *The Wizard of Oz*). Maybe this comes from internal recognition. As Waite asks, "What is that within us which does sound a trumpet and all that is lower in our nature rises in response—almost in a moment, almost in the twinkling of an eye?"[4]

I struggled for many years to write a novel. All the while I struggled, I saw visions of a Tarot deck. I decided to work on designing this deck, thinking that I would "get it out of my head" so I could focus on the novel, which I thought would be my "actual" great work. I denigrated the deck as a distraction, but because it wouldn't leave my brain, I set the novel aside and worked on it instead. It wasn't until the Tarot deck was near completion that I realized *it* was the novel I tried so hard to write. My own Judgment card moment in that creative Fool's journey was realizing I was on my right creation path all along. Moreover, it was a call to action that my creative work was in the realm of metaphysics.

Judgment is also the point in our journey when we suddenly get a glimpse of the next chapter. The truth revealed in the Judgment card differs from other revelatory cards—such as the Moon, which is often truth in retrospect—because Judgment peers into the future. Many of my clients receive this card when they are looking for clarification on their chosen career or relationships. It's a sign that says, "Embark on this." When we reflect on Judgment cards in our own journeys, they signify points in our lives that included a call to a new adventure. In other circumstances, it can mean a decision needs to be made. In this situation, that decision will have a great enough impact to change the future of the path, but it doesn't quite signify the end. The end is still to come. The Judgment card may also catch us when we are inches from the finish line but may be tempted to give in to exhaustion. Judgment asks us, "You've come all this way. Are you really going to quit now?" It reminds us of our first calling, why we started this mess of a journey in the first place. It also reminds us that our destinies are often rooted in specific choices from the beginning until the very end and if we are going to complete what we've started, we must make the choice to do so even when it seems the end is in sight.

21. THE WORLD

The woman depicted in the World card symbolizes the end of the Fool's journey. The credits roll, the chapter ends. Perhaps there is a sequel coming, or perhaps this is the last we'll see of the Fool. The World represents an ending, but one more satisfying than traumatic. The work that the Fool sets out to do is completed in accordance with the Universe's desire.

The World card is also a hallmark of a new journey about to start. Maybe this marks the end of the Fool's mortal life, and if so, it represents the Fool's transformation into a new incarnation, be it in an afterlife, a reincarnation, or a physical transformation into soil and minerals that feed trees and flowers. The World keeps turning, and so the Fool keeps moving, too.

The ritual of graduation is a perfect example of a World card moment. An educational journey is complete and the degree achieved. Most people would likely describe the journey through high school, college, or further degrees as full of the peaks and valleys, characters and obstacles that the Fool experiences in the Major Arcana. Once, one of my clients recently asked if her upcoming business trip to South America would be her last to the continent. She pulled the World card from the deck. The message seemed to be that it would indeed be her final trip to South America. The idea didn't upset her, as she felt for some time that she wanted a change in her career, but she wanted to make sure the work she had started would reach a healthy conclusion. Receiving a card that signified a healthy, whole resolution gave her the final push to travel and complete the necessary work.

When we receive the World card, one door is closing, but another will soon open. The Major Arcana reminds us that nothing is ever truly gone from our world. Nothing ends; it merely transforms. The difference in the World card from other transformation or conclusion cards is the sign of ascension within it. When we receive the World card, we are "leveling up." The level we have been working on so diligently has concluded, and we are free to see what else we are capable of doing and being. Oswald Wirth points out that the character in the center of the World card is like "a squirrel who makes its cage go round."[5] It also reminds us that even in death we don't leave this world; we merely change forms. We are it, and it is us.

And the world keeps turning . . .

DISCOVERING YOUR FOOL'S JOURNEY

Our lives are comprised of stories within chapters within tomes. We have all experienced the Fool's journey over the course of our whole lives, and we may have also experienced the journey over a few months, a week, or even a day. Recognizing your journey through the archetypes of the Major Arcana is a primer step in reading your own Tarot. This first exercise will explore how the Fool's journey has manifested in your experiences.

Your Fool's Journey

Think of your entire life up to this point as one long trip through the Major Arcana, with you as the Fool. In the following exercise, make notes about how each Tarot card has appeared in your personal Fool's journey. Who from your life fits the scenario? How would you describe them and their role in your life?

For example, for the Empress card, you would list people who have served as maternal figures for you. In this exercise, do not focus on times when you have been the card figure for someone else. We will explore that in the subsequent exercise. Let this first one be about other people and experiences that have impacted your journey.

Some cards may seem quite familiar to experiences you've had. Others may seem foreign. Some may have had great influence, while others had a smaller impact. You may not have experienced all of these yet. If this is the case for some of the characters, write "not yet." Chances are good that you will think of an example later, but even if you don't, the practice leaves room for recognizing these embodied cards as they materialize.

You may find one person or example fits into more than one Major Arcana category, even several times. It is perfectly fine to list the same person or example more than once. Some people or situations make very deep impressions—deeper than a single Tarot card can encapsulate!

It is also okay to stretch these definitions. Perhaps you didn't know your father, but you had an older sister who acted as a co-parent to your mother. If this feels like an appropriate definition for the Emperor in your Fool's journey, write it down. You are not being tested. There is no wrong answer.

As you are also likely to notice, real-life Fool's journeys are rarely in the same chronological order as they are written in the Major Arcana. Most of our journeys loop around, double back, jump forward, or travel through these thresholds numerous times. Do not try to force your personal life journey into Tarot's chronological order. Simply write down examples as best as you can.

- ◆ The Magician: An influential mentor or teacher

- ◆ The High Priestess: A spiritual advisor or moment of profound inspiration

- ◆ The Empress: Your mother or a maternal figure

- ◆ The Emperor: Your father or a paternal figure

- ◆ The Hierophant: An institutional figurehead

- ◆ The Lovers: A new love—a romantic or platonic relationship with a person, or a vocation

- ◆ The Chariot: A time when you set out on your own or took control of yourself or a situation

- ◆ Strength: A time you demonstrated personal strength

- ◆ The Hermit: A time you gained insight through a period of solitude or via an unassuming person

- ◆ Wheel of Fortune: A time when you changed your circumstances through choice, determination, seizing an opportunity or otherwise

- ◆ Justice: A time you were rightfully rewarded or punished for words or deeds

- ◆ The Hanged Man: A time when you were stuck or left without choice

- ◆ Death: A time when you suffered a great loss

- ◆ Temperance: A time of compromise or attaining balance, and/or "coming back to life"

- ◆ The Devil: An enemy—either an outside person or situation, or an internal conflict

- ◆ The Tower: A great collapse—when something fell apart suddenly, or a great "aha!" moment

- ◆ The Star: A hope or dream—perhaps a time when you chose to hope, dream, or act on faith

- ◆ The Moon: A great mystery or secret you personally keep or kept or a time when a mystery was revealed for you

- ◆ The Sun: A time you embraced pure confidence and joy

- ◆ Judgment: A time when you heard a call to action or made a big decision that dramatically changed your life

- ◆ The World: The end of a chapter in your life

A Journey in a Day

Reflect on your day as a complete journey of the Fool. Using only the Major Arcana, draw five cards and lay them in a line. From left to right, these cards represent the following:

1. Morning

2. Midday

3. Early Afternoon

4. Late Afternoon

5. Evening

Here is a sample reading:

1. Morning—The Empress: My husband and I do not yet have children, but I did ensure we both ate a healthy breakfast. We also talked about finances and household needs. It was a nurturing, nourishing morning.

2. Midday—Judgment: I had a meeting with a colleague at which we discussed plans for a large function. Toward the end of the meeting, she said she had an idea for me, which spoke to an opportunity I'd been looking for.

3. Early Afternoon—Strength: I became very sleepy after lunch, so I did my best to tap personal strength in order to keep awake without coffee. This involved getting away from my desk and taking a walk. Considering I've only recently given up caffeine, it took great strength!

4. Late Afternoon—The Emperor: In the afternoon, another colleague and I worked on some institutional care taking, strengthening a program we did not start but inherited and now manage. We also swapped stories about our fathers in the middle of it. Very appropriate!

5. The Evening—The Lovers: Friday nights are sanctioned for my husband and me to spend together. As today is Friday, our evening was spent harvesting a little quality time!

The goal of the exercise is to help you become familiar with the Major Arcana in the context of more routine occurrences than significant life events. In your self-readings, they will manifest as both. In your own reading, what did you learn about the cards pulled? What did you learn about your day in retrospect? Did any smaller moments actually hold more punch than you realized? Did anything about this reading surprise you?

Your Part in the Journeys of Others

As the World card reminds us, we don't operate in vacuums. We are all Fools on our own journeys, intertwined with the journeys of others. Throughout our lives, we will play the same archetypal roles that others have played for us.

In this exercise, do your best to identify instances when you were one of these archetypes to another person. Set aside concerns about ego projection. Others may not see you in their journeys as you see yourself, but that is not a problem. Do your best to draw conclusions, and don't worry whether the other person would agree with that assessment. The ultimate goal here is to better understand both sides of the Major Arcana of the Tarot, and these notes are for you alone.

Write down your answers to the following questions. If you cannot think of an example, write "not sure" or not yet."

- ◆ The Magician: When have you acted as a teacher or mentor to another person?

- ◆ The High Priestess: When have you acted as an unusual advisor or inspired another person?

- The Empress: When have you been a mother or a maternal figure?

- The Emperor: When have you been a father or a paternal figure?

- The Hierophant: When have you been part of a dominant authority, perhaps religious, institutional, corporate, or some other kind of organization?

- The Lovers: When have you been the object of someone's affection or perhaps introduced another to something or someone they truly love?

- The Chariot: When have you been the force that encourages someone to take control or when were you under the control of someone else?

- Strength: When were you a source of strength for another person?

- The Hermit: When did you act as a beacon of wisdom for someone else? When did you provide solace in privacy?

- Wheel of Fortune: When have you aided in changing circumstances or provided an opportunity for another person?

- Justice: When have you provided "what someone deserved" either through accolades, punishment, or otherwise?

- The Hanged Man: When have you prevented another person from acting according to their will?

- Death: When were you the source of death, loss, or a significant ending?

- Temperance: When have you created restrictions or balance for another person or situation or helped to give them new life?

- The Devil: When have you been an obstacle or enemy for another person or situation?

- The Tower: When have you been the source of upheaval or collapse?

- The Star: When have you provided hope?

- The Moon: When have you revealed a secret, particularly one that impacts someone else?

- The Sun: When have you inspired optimism, courage, or confidence in another person?

- Judgment: When have you provided a call to action or put a confusing situation in perspective?

- The World: When have you provided closure?

Again, do your best to find examples of yourself in these roles. We will all fulfill most if not all of these roles at some point. Sometimes, we may not even be aware of it when it happens. This and the previous exercise can both be wonderfully reflective as an annual practice.

The Roles We Play

This next exercise will further explore your Major Arcana roles in the journeys of others. Particularly if you struggled with finding these roles in the previous exercise, this one may help you identify them.

Using only the Major Arcana, randomly draw four cards and lay them face up in a line. From left to right, here is the significance of each card:

1. The largest role you play to others

2. The smallest role you play to others

3. How you challenge others

4. How you bless others

My own reading went as follows:

1. The largest role I play to others: The Moon—Much of my work involves making sense of mysteries, such as writing books about Tarot! However, since the Moon can also mean creating mystery, it might behoove me to make sure I'm not coming across as aloof.

2. The smallest role I play to others: The Sun—If we consider the Sun as jovial and joyful, it's possible I have room to bring more of that to others. I am very work-focused. Maybe there is more room for play. Then again, the bright light of the sun can burn, while moonlight is gentler. Maybe a gentler light is something I offer.

3. How I challenge others: Judgment—If we see judgment as a call to action, that makes sense to me, as I frequently organize activists and rally them for the work. I also facilitate decision making within my Coven and day job. The other side of the Judgment card may encourage me to be careful of being judgmental of others.

4. How I bless others: The Tower—The Tower seems like an odd blessing, but if there is a blessing in knocking down an existing structure, this might be it! I do like challenging norms and breaking rules. Perhaps I encourage others to do the same.

Were you surprised by any of your cards? Remember, this exercise is only a snapshot of your life at this moment. Your roles for others will change, but you will notice certain patterns over time. This exercise can be repeated once every few months. Doing it more often than that will likely seem contradictory and may be confusing. Don't forget to take notes and compare new readings with past ones.

THREE

COURT CARDS

The sixteen cards most commonly labeled Page, Knight, Queen, and King are known as the Tarot Court. They are found in the four suits of the Minor Arcana. The Court cards represent individuals in our lives, roles we play in the lives of others, or aspects of ourselves. Sometimes, they appear as messengers. Other times, they represent conflict. Some may manifest in your readings as lessons or blessings. In my self-readings, the Court cards have provided some of the most poignant and synchronistic experiences.

These may sound similar to the Major Arcana. My experience with the Court cards has shown them to be more fluid than the Majors. While more than one Court card in a reading can certainly signify more than one person or influence in a situation, they are equally as likely to represent more than one aspect to a person or influence. While naturally this could be true for Major Arcana cards in some readings, I've found this fluidity to be a bit more common among the Court cards. In addition, the Court cards signify the diversity of roles we play in our current lives, as opposed to the Major Arcana, which is more likely to illustrate roles we play over the course of our entire lives.

Who Are These Characters?

At one time, the Court cards may have represented common societal hierarchy: The Kings were the grand rulers. The Queens held some authority, but not as much as the Kings. The Knights were meant as an elite, protective force, but without the leadership qualities of the Kings and Queens. The Pages were subservient, possibly able to become Knights themselves one day, but working in a service role in the meantime. In the twenty-first century these roles are mostly defunct, especially those of the King and the Queen. The idea of a King or Queen may still encourage leadership, but we can fortunately view a Queen with as much power and prestige as a King. A Knight can still mean a protective force, and Pages reflect a service role, but while Tarot has historically defined them both as male, these cards can and often are depicted as any gender.

Gender in the Court Cards

We can find aspects of ourselves within each Court card no matter how we identify ourselves gender-wise, power-wise, etc. For the sake of continuity I will refer to the cards using their traditional gender associations, but, as with the Major Arcana, the true nature of each Court card is beyond gender. (The Knights and Pages in the RWS deck are rather ambiguous in their gender in the first place. Who can really tell what is beneath all that armor or pantaloons, anyway?)

As you work with your self-readings, you may find a Court card that you don't feel corresponds with your gender identity routinely appears as a symbol for you, and yet it will be absolutely accurate. Be open to unusual gender pairings in cards meant to represent yourself. These surprising cards can provide wonderful insight. I self-identify as female, yet I often find the King of Wands exemplifies my position in a situation. When I receive either a King or a Queen in a reading, I see it as representative of the greatest potential I have at any given moment. If it is a Queen, it encourages me to draw on natural strengths. If it is a King, it encourages me to make choices that perhaps don't come quite as naturally to me.

Nonconforming Gender in the Court Cards

The traditional Tarot has a history of highly gendered characters that can exclude people who don't identify with a binary gender. Gender nonconforming (GNC) Tarot readers have shared with me that they frequently view the Court cards as aspects of self, assigning different qualities to each based on what they personally understand as masculine or feminine.[1] One GNC reader said they see a King as a sign to be more direct and a Queen as a sign to be more cautious. Another GNC reader mentioned they remove gender from the cards altogether and associate Court cards with actions and events. Others mentioned that they forgo decks with strong gender propensity and use decks with fewer or no gender associations at all, such as decks that depict the Court cards with animals, fantasy symbols, or even just colors and shapes. No matter how you personally identify gender-wise, trying out decks with different gender depictions or none at all will enhance your understanding of Tarot. The exercises later in this chapter are built to help people of all genders connect with aspects of the Court cards.

Know the Old, but Embrace the New

While you are exploring Tarot through self-reading, the cards will eventually manifest and share their own messages with you in their own ways. Yet knowing some of the older interpretations is helpful. Our world may be reconsidering gender roles and identity, but the Spirit of Tarot still carries several centuries of a specific culture's gender associations that may seem archaic, sexist, or binary-bound. This doesn't mean we have to cling to these associations. If thousands of people over hundreds of years dropped primary yellow into an ocean of white paint (imagine this is a white paint that never dries), there would be an ocean of very yellow paint. But say one day the descendants of those people decided they wanted a green ocean and began dropping blue paint into the mix. Eventually the paint-ocean would turn green, but for quite a bit of time yellow would show through. This doesn't mean that the paint is inherently yellow—it is simply responding to what was put into it, initially. It will continue to respond to what is placed into it in the future and will eventually be a very green shade of green. Tarot is no different. It is not inherently sexist or gendered, but tones that may feel as such may surface in readings once in a while. Understanding this may be helpful to working with the cards, but know that we as readers contribute to the tones of Tarot for future readers and have the power to contribute our own associations to the collective Tarot Spirit.

Traditional Meanings of the Court Cards

The list below is a collection of some of the more traditional meanings for the Court cards. Let these help you become better oriented with them. If they resonate with you, that's wonderful! If they don't, let them go. It is not necessary to memorize them.[2]

- ◆ The Kings: Patriarchal rulers, masculine. These are individuals at the height of their power and talent. They represent authority, dexterity, or depth of their suit.

- ◆ The Queens: Matriarchal rules, feminine. Like the Kings, they are the supreme authority of their specific suit. If you have a history with

Western playing cards, you may find that your natural instinct is to place the King in a stronger position than the Queen. If this is how you view the cards, it is not wrong. I know of a reader who is very much a feminist, but in her Tarot readings she associates the Kings as more powerful than the Queens because this reader is also a regular poker player. Many of today's readers find the Kings and Queens are on equal footing with regards to authority and represent the subtle nuances between masculine and feminine energies.

♦ The Knights: The warriors, seekers, deliverers. The knights are in motion and represent "going for" something. They haven't achieved the status of the Queen or the King, but it is possible to achieve that status if the forces of the Universe work in their favor. They represent the doers of this world. They can also represent conflict, battle, and protection.

♦ The Pages: The beginners, the children of promise. The Page is the learning character. They can represent youth, but they also represent being new at something or a new thing being introduced. The Page can also be considered a Messenger.

What's Your Role in Court?

Review the traditional meanings of the Court cards. Do any particularly resonate with you? If using these associations to define the largest role you play in your present life, what might it be? Would you define your general current life role as a King, Queen, Knight, or Page? Strive for honesty. Do not falsely humble yourself or overinflate your role, either. This is only for you, so you have the liberty to be fully honest without others questioning you!

We all embody all Tarot roles at some point. What Court cards have you embodied in the past? What Court cards feel foreign to you and your role? Are there aspects of the Court cards that you would ideally like to embody? Are there any you'd rather not embody? Make notes about your thoughts in your Tarot journal.

A Description of the Minor Arcana

Tarot's Court cards are part of the Minor Arcana. As mentioned above, the Minor Arcana is broken into four suits, most commonly identified as Pentacles, Swords, Wands, and Cups. There are numerous variations of these suits among different decks out there: disks or coins for Pentacles, knives or scimitars for Swords, rods for Wands, and chalices or bowls for Cups. These are all valid, but I will refer to them in their forms of Pentacles, Swords, Wands, and Cups solely for the sake of continuity.

Prior to the twentieth century, the Minor Arcana was completely composed of faceless images, similar to the Western playing card suits of Diamonds, Spades, Clubs, and Hearts. In the early 1900s, Pamela Colman Smith revolutionized the Tarot by creating character-illustrated scenes for the Minor Arcana. Waite did not believe the Minor Arcana cards had meanings equal in power to those of the Major Arcana.[3] I don't agree. While the Major Arcana certainly represents pivotal points of the personal journey, the Minor Arcana and its Court cards highlight the depth and beauty of everyday moments. A brief but meaningful conversation with a classmate on a late night can carry as much presence on the soul as the graduation ceremony. In this lens, the Minor Arcana is anything but minor.

The four suits are most commonly associated with four elemental presences, as follows:

- ◆ Pentacles—Earth

- ◆ Swords—Air

- ◆ Wands—Fire

- ◆ Cups—Water

Again, these associations vary. Swords or their equivalent sometimes represent fire, while wands may represent air. I will use the more common interpretations mentioned above. If your preferred deck offers different associations, you may want to make a translation page in your Tarot journal. The elementals represent energies and influences. We will look at examples in the next section. The Court cards reflect how these different influences emerge through a person's roles, personality traits, or experiences. In this section, we'll walk through the different elementals and explore some ways they are revealed through these lenses. We will also explore interpretations of reversed cards—when a card appears upside down in a reading.

PENTACLES (COINS/DISKS)

Element: Earth

Significance: Work, material goods, health, strength, money

Realm: The body

The King of Pentacles

KING of PENTACLES.

Character: Master of material goods, a wealthy person of masculine persuasion. A paternal figure who provides richly for the family or community. A boss. This may not be the most effusive or romantic card, but it provides the most material comfort. A healthy, comfortable person.

Traits: Loving and affectionate, but through practical means. Sensible. Devoted. Generous, but not without boundaries. Someone in good health.

Experience: The epitome of living the good life. Strength in finance, solid ground. The ship finally coming in, the desired comforts achieved. Strong body and mind.

Reversed: Cold and withholding, ungenerous and unloving, a person not living the good life at all. This King may have lost his title—perhaps success overinflated his ego and eventually eroded his power. It may be someone who falsely boasts of their success or wealth. As reversed cards can indicate secrets, this card in reverse may mean hidden fortune or talents. As a rule, any Kings or Queens in reverse may suggest that the querent has far more potential than they're willing to live up to. The King in reverse may mean poor health.

woody

The Queen of Pentacles

Character: A person of feminine persuasion, also a master/mistress of material goods. A person of deep intelligence. A healthy person. A mother or maternal figure, equally as generous as the king. A productive, successful person, perhaps the boss of a company or corporation.

Traits: Health, fertility, prudent with money; possibly one to place money or practicality over emotion or the well-being of others. Detached affection—showing love through gift giving. May extract or demand more resources. Shows a desire for life's finer things.

QUEEN of PENTACLES

Experience: Motherhood or parenthood. Luxury, comfort, privilege, possibly living outside of one's means. Feeling good about oneself in body and soul.

Reversed: Like the King, a reversed Queen of Pentacles may be withholding resources. She may not be at the pinnacle of her power yet. She may be selling herself short. Her power may have weakened. Her health may be poor. She may harbor doubts about her abilities.

The Knight of Pentacles

Character: The deliverer—bringer of opportunity and stability. All of the knights are doers and bringers, but the Knight of Pentacles is the consistent one. Although slower than the other Knights, the Knight of Pentacles is the most accurate. A hard worker, but one who paces themselves. Can be practical to the point of being boring. The Knight may be seeking to test or prove his strength against competitors or against his own personal limits.

Tee?

KNIGHT of PENTACLES.

Traits: Acts on logic before emotion, follows a careful plan of action. Gentle, methodical, focused. Some might say dull, but none would say lazy. Someone who is seeking better health—either through medicine or a health and/or fitness plan.

Experience: Hard, focused work. Minimizing distractions, frugality. Approaching long-term goals. Less about dreaming big, more about planning big. Becoming stronger.

Reversed: Stuck, perhaps even lazy. The symbolic horse may have gone lame, or perhaps the Knight lacks the true drive to complete the task. It may indicate a false deal, or one that is permanently shelved. It may also indicate a setback in financial planning or some sort of loss. The reversed Knight of Pentacles is a sign that something must change in order to go forward.

The Page of Pentacles

Tee?

PAGE of PENTACLES.

Character: Someone new to a job or career field, or perhaps someone who recently inherited some money. Someone learning the very basic or practical tricks of a trade; a modern embodiment might be an office intern. The Page of Pentacles may be a wealthy person, but the potential for the person to grow into something greater is huge. Someone learning to understand the body and its needs and impulses, such as a toddler learning to walk or use the toilet. As a messenger, the Page has helpful, practical information.

Traits: Studious, industrious, earnest, honest. May not be perfectly skilled but pays excellent attention. Open and willing mind, energetic body.

Experience: A new opportunity, perhaps one that will foster fantastic returns. A small but key investment.

Reversed: Poverty—material, emotional, or spiritual. Pages in reverse can indicate withholding truth or outright dishonesty. Whenever a Page appears in reverse, there is more to the story that needs to be uncovered. It may indicate minor health problems, perhaps those that are being ignored.

SWORDS

Element: **Air**

Significance: **Communication, thought, conflict, movement**

Realm: **The mind**

The King of Swords

Charlie

Character: A masculine person of shrewd authority. This King does not mince words. He does not compromise. He makes swift decisions and definitive judgments. His word is final. The King of Swords can also be a great protector, like a master bodyguard. He thinks deeply but makes decisions quickly. He commands respect—even fear.

Traits: Decisive, cold, and calculated, logical and intelligent. Forthright, even blunt. Possibly angry, possessive, even abusive.

Experience: Making quick but firm decisions—often from a seat of power over others or over ourselves. Sometimes, the King of Swords can signify toxic situations.

KING of SWORDS.

Reversed: Indecision. A softening of authority. A weak person or position. If abuse or unkindness is present, the King of Swords may represent the culprit being unaware of their actions or determined to keep them secret. It can also represent a drop in personal defenses or no longer being able to depend on another person for protection. A reversed King of Swords may mean an undermining of authority.

The Queen of Swords

QUEEN of SWORDS.

Character: A feminine person of shrewd decisiveness. She is decisive, quick to choose and judge. She does not play favorites. The King and Queen of Swords are the lawyers and lawmakers of the world. They both define and enforce the rules. Being of the mind, the Queen is a strong communicator, possibly a spokesperson. Sometimes, she manifests as a sad or hurt woman. Both the King and Queen can mean an angry or vengeful person. The Queen is not the warm and friendly presence more commonly associated with the Queen of Pentacles, but she can be humorous.

Traits: Austerity, leadership, enforcement of rules. Frankness and fairness, but also coldness. Strength in words, but ones that are carefully chosen. Determination, focus, fortitude.

Experience: The uncomfortable position of making tough decisions with full logic, not sentimentality. Making deep sacrifices for the greater good; drawing boundaries, enforcing rules, leaving little room for negotiation.

Reversed: Lax rules, inattentive leadership. Perhaps some room for negotiation. A past injury may be forgiven, but never forgotten. There may be irrational actions, thoughts, or decisions. A Queen of Swords in reverse can also indicate back-biting. She may represent an illusion of an enemy rather than an actual one. Also, like the King, the Queen of Swords in reverse represents someone being hurtful and not being aware of the damage they are doing. For ourselves, it can indicate a call for self-awareness of our words and actions to others.

The Knight of Swords

Character: The Knight of Swords is the fastest of all of the Knights, but he is not always the most graceful or accurate. Sometimes, this Knight moves so fast he doesn't even pay mindful attention to the goal he's ultimately after. Yet, he is completely fearless. Can mean a nefarious person.

Traits: Aim and focus and a refusal to quit until the job is done. Clear and direct communication. Potentially acting before thinking as a default mode of operation. A desire to be a hero, possibly a martyrdom complex.

Experience: A Knight of Swords can and does often indicate conflict. But it can also mean a welcome breath of fresh air in a stagnant place. It may mean being forced to make a decision when there isn't time to think about options. It can indicate circumstances changing quickly and dramatically. A time to champion on behalf of others without considering yourself.

Reversed: A warning not to ride so quickly into battle. The card may represent opposition backing down. It can indicate a loss of direction in projects or plans. It may also be a call to us to stop pursuing a specific endeavor. The Knight of Swords encourages us to soften our words and ease up on our actions. It may ask us to reconsider what we are fighting for.

The Page of Swords

Character: Someone gruff, grumpy, possibly mildly annoying but not someone who is a threat. The Page of Swords could be friendly competition, but competition that should not be taken too flippantly. Like the other Pages, the Page of Swords may be small but has the potential to grow into something greater. The danger of the Page of Swords is that he should never be underestimated, yet he often is. As a messenger card, the Page of Swords carries a particular vital piece of information.

Traits: Feisty, short-tempered, possibly quick to battle over small things. Honest, but may not have the whole truth of a situation. Likes to pick sides, but doesn't always have a strong sense of loyalty. Quick to point out the obvious. Not particularly tactful.

Experience: Angry words, or a swift message. The Page of Swords is a conflict card, but a minor one. It can indicate something of a scuffle that could escalate if it's not given proper attention and intention. The Page of Swords may be a reminder not to ignore a seemingly trivial situation. It may indicate needing to make a minor decision.

Reversed: The Page of Swords in reverse may ease some fears. It can mean that the threatening shadow on the wall is simply a shadow. There may be dishonesty present—either for yourself, for others, or maybe someone has been dishonest with you. Lastly, like any Swords card in reverse, it may indicate undermining. Like a pebble in a shoe, something seemingly small may be making you quite uncomfortable. This can be a warning sign to stop and ask ourselves if we're truly happy with certain aspects of a situation.

WANDS

Element: Fire

Significance: Creation, creativity, sexuality, inspiration, drive, production, invention

Realm: Spirit

The King of Wands — *clay*

Character: A male-identified master of creation. He has good intentions but can be severe. In the RWS deck, his garment carries the symbol of the lion, which may connect to the astrological sign of Leo, a fire-sign ruled by the sun. The card can mean great authority, such as a seat in government or on a board of directors. It may suggest he is comfortable enough with his abilities that he doesn't worry about how things will manifest—they simply will! On a counter note, the King of Wands may have gotten a little flippant and could stand to take things a little more seriously. The King of Wands can indicate a person who is interested in a sexual relationship but not a long-term romance.

KING of WANDS

Traits: Courageous and confident, honest and conscientious. Charisma and charm. A strong moral stance.

Experience: It can indicate a revitalization of chemistry and drive—for a relationship, a career pursuit, or otherwise. A major opportunity may be presenting itself and should be given serious consideration.

Reversed: Something may be incomplete. There may be more work to be done. It may indicate overconfidence. Someone you admire may not be all that they seem. Perhaps you are the one who is overconfident.

But it may also represent "settling." Are you selling yourself a little short? Is your full potential being overlooked? Perhaps the anticipation of connection is overshadowing actual connection (This is a card that can indicate online dating gone awry. Maybe the outcome did not meet the expectation?). It may also represent someone who is not as fully invested in a person or a project as they may appear. Maybe you are the one who is not as interested as perhaps you are letting others believe.

The Queen of Wands

me
—Alice

QUEEN of WANDS.

Character: Like the King, the Queen of Wands is accomplished at her craft, whatever that craft may be. When I produced my deck[4], my collaborator and I photographed an accomplished artist in her home studio, surrounded by a life's work of paintings. Sitting regally, surrounded by her beloved creations, she was the living embodiment of the Queen of Wands.

Traits: An energizing force—creatively and sexually. Confidence; a friendly nature. Like the King, she embodies fully living the spirit of fire. Passionate. Quick to anger, quick to laugh. Spirited and not always focused, but inspiring nonetheless.

Experience: Success in undertakings and enterprises. Birthing a dream into reality. An adventure in banking, agriculture, art, and money.

Reversed: It's possible you're not feeling your full sexy swagger when you receive the Queen of Wands reversed. Maybe you're not showing off your beautiful colors. Creative potential may have been lost. The zeal for your work may have slowed. Like the King reversed, it may indicate incompletion. It may also encourage giving less credence to flattery.

Both the King and Queen of Wands in reverse may indicate a loss of confidence.

The Knight of Wands

Character: A young or young-spirited person. A new person in town or someone who isn't likely to stick around for long, as this Knight often precedes transition. Like the Knight of Swords, the Knight of Wands is swift. The Knight of Wands moves with haste, but not always with accuracy. Capable of creating conflict or rivalry, likely because this Knight draws many suitors and can inspire envy.

Traits: Excitement, passion. The need to roam. Potentially disruptive, in a class clown kind of way. General feelings of unrest, possibly willing to upset the status quo.

KNIGHT of WANDS.

Experience: A sudden burst of inspiration. A time to pursue a particular dream. Knights frequently indicate travel. This Knight suggests a spontaneous journey, maybe a creative pilgrimage or retreat. The Knight of Wands may indicate a sudden storm of passion such as an irresistible tumble in the sheets.

Reversed: A lack of confidence. Waning interest in a project. Flames of chemistry fading in a relationship. It may indicate that someone is not pulling their weight. The positive thing about the reversed Knight of Wands, or any reversed Knight, is that it doesn't signify a dead-end. The passion of the Knight of Wands can be reignited with the right focus and determination.

The Page of Wands

PAGE of WANDS.

Character: A child or child-like character. Someone with a partially formed idea, but one with the potential to expand beautifully. Someone with a crush on someone else. A person with raw talent but little training. This Page represents an internal messenger, encouraging listening to ideas rattling around in your head.

Traits: Emerging qualities of self. Supportive of others. Positivity. Enthusiasm.

Experience: If the Wands are a suit of creation, the Page of Wands might be a blank canvas or document. It's the start of something potentially big. The Page of Wands may indicate simmering chemistry between you and someone else. Like blowing on coals under kindling, the promise of larger flames is present but may need a little encouragement. It can indicate an announcement.

Reversed: A suggestion to approach a project or situation from a new angle, particularly if you're feeling stuck. It may mean a lack of honesty about true abilities. Others may not be as impressed with you or your work as you previously believed. In love, it's possibly mistaking fleeting attention for deeper interest—a spark extinguished before it ever caught fire. This reversed Page may represent another person having little to add to your life. It may represent bad news.

CUPS

Element: Water

Significance: Emotions, relationships, family, ancestry, inheritance

Realm: The heart

The King of Cups *Evan?*

KING of CUPS.

Character: A masculine person ready for commitment, parenthood, responsibility. An honest person. Kings of Cups are philosophers, idealists, and teachers. Wherever he goes, his heart leads. He has probably suffered heartbreak already in his life and knows not to waste true love when he finds it. He is someone who is ready for commitment—be it to a relationship, an endeavor, or a calling.

Traits: In touch with one's emotions, maturity. An open and available heart. Ready to dig deeper, unafraid of the unknown. Willing and ready for love. Whimsical, philosophical, idealistic, dramatic.

Experience: Falling in love, making a commitment. Embarking on a vocational calling. An opportunity linked to your true desires. Something truly fulfilling.

Reversed: A lack of investment without return, depression, futility. May also represent repressed or secret feelings. If this card represents you, it might suggest abdication of responsibility or avoiding commitment. If it represents another person, they may not be as committed as you might hope.

The Queen of Cups

QUEEN of CUPS.

Character: A feminine person ready for love and/or commitment. Her heart is firm and strong. She is a willing partner, a loving parent, and, like the King, she is devoted to what she loves. She is often in service to others. Pulling the Queen of Cups may represent having found your true calling. The Queen of Cups can be linked to fame or renown—for better or worse!

Gina

Traits: Fairness, honesty, kindness, devotion. Care and attention, to the self or to others. Loving intelligence and practical wisdom. Powerful intuition and/or psychic ability. – *Auntie Sue*

Experience: Garnering obedience from others, particularly younger family members. Getting married and/or experiencing motherhood. Psychic premonitions.

– *Jen*
– *Gina*
– *Auntie Sue*
– *Mother*

Reversed: There is a sense of something "not being right." The feminine cards are often linked to intuitive impulses, and so a reversed one may indicate a call to pay attention to feelings being a bit "off." If something doesn't feel quite right, the Queen of Cups reversed suggests paying attention to that feeling. Like the King of Cups in reverse, the reversed Water Queen can suggest depression or repressed feelings. It might signify a lack of honesty, either with the self or others. Lastly, it may suggest a lack of romantic or emotional interest or secrets being kept from you. It can also mean notoriety or cruelty.

The Knight of Cups

Character: The Knight of Cups is the great seeker of love. This Knight carries his heart in his hands, both offering and following it, and forever searching. This could be a romantic, vocational, or other sort of pursuit. Yet while the Knight of Cups has great heart, this Knight is not always accurate. Sometimes emotion will override logic, or the Knight will be so swept up in desire they won't pause to decide if they only want for the sake of wanting. Still, this Knight is a skilled seeker. Eventually, this Knight will find what they're looking for. This card can also suggest a traveler or a merchant.

Traits: Devotion, magnetism. Idealism. Indulgent in fantasy. Slightly unfulfilled. Possibly lonely.

Experience: The Knight of Cups is less about going into battle and more about completing a quest, the quest for love in particular. This may be seeking new love, rekindling an old love, or perhaps seeking friendship. The Knight of Cups may also be seeking forgiveness. Part of the Knight's journey is learning to share and connect with other people. This Knight is connected to seeking the Holy Grail—embarking on a journey to uncover great mysteries of Spirit.

Reversed: Abandoning a quest. A lack of enthusiasm. A lack of hope. The wrong time to look for love. Others not being forthright with their true feelings about a situation. Someone who may not be as interested in you as they say they are. More sinister meanings may include lies, slander, fraud, or blackmail.

The Page of Cups

Character: The Page of Cups represents a youthful heart. A pure and honest person who gives without ego or expectation. They mean well but may be a tad naïve. As a messenger, the Page offers truth and honesty. Because of its connections with water, it may be a message of love. This Page may be a student.

Traits: A kind friend; a democratic mind. Sympathy and empathy. Tendency to please and to make things or certain people appear better than they are in reality. An openness and curiosity about sex. Focused and studious.

Experience: Work, application, reflection, observation. Taking on a new job or line of work. Using encouraging words to build up others. Commitment, possibly a proposal of marriage. Seduction. It may also represent a return to a childlike heart or meeting a person we can love as though we've never been hurt. A Page of Cups moment might be a child drawing a picture for their mother, or the first time two people, newly in love, touch hands. It has been known to represent the birth of something—a child, or a relationship.

Reversed: A false start to a relationship. Miscommunication. A sign to focus on improving communication with others. A suggestion to reach out to people you've not seen in awhile. If you've been investing substantial time or emotional energy into others, this card may be a suggestion to pull back some, as that energy may not be returned.

Who Are the Court Cards in Your Life?

Reading through these descriptions, you may have already associated some of these characters with people you know, roles you hold, or certain aspects of yourself. Like the Major Arcana, we will experience all of these individuals and hold all of these roles ourselves at some point.

Our Personal Court Characters

Reflect on your journey, making notes in your journal if it's helpful. If you were to write a script of the life you've lead, both past and present, who would be the major characters? Instead of listing their names, list the role they play or once played in your life. For example, if you once had a boyfriend named William, instead of writing down "William," you might write down "The Boyfriend," or "The Lover." Be sure to choose roles from your current life as well as your past, including both positive and negative experiences. I asked Julie, who had little experience with Tarot, to try the exercise.

Julie's list is as follows:

The Mother	The Teacher
The Sibling	The Cheater
The Father	The Spouse
The Cousin	The Child
The Friend	The Employer
The Caretaker	The Leader
The Lover	The Mentor
The Enemy	The Assistant or "Helper"

Next, remove the sixteen Court cards from your deck and study them. Based on the images of your deck's Court cards, which would you connect to these roles? Maybe your Queen of Swords looks particularly stern, so you would connect them with a strict employer. If your King of Wands is a jolly character, maybe you'll connect them with a boisterous friend. Allow your imagination to make the primary connections. If you get stuck, draw from the descriptions in the previous section if they are helpful, but allow yourself to form natural associations even if they don't reflect traditional interpretations. Make notes of your associations next to your list.

Julie's associations are below:

The Mother: The Page of Swords

The Sibling: The Page of Wands

The Father: The King of Cups

The Cousin: The King of Pentacles

The Friend: The Knight of Wands

The Caretaker: The Knight of Swords

The Lover: The Queen of Wands

The Enemy: The King of Swords

The Teacher: The Queen of Swords

The Cheater: The Page of Pentacles

The Spouse: The Queen of Cups

The Child: The Knight of Cups

The Employer: The Knight of Pentacles

The Leader: The Queen of Pentacles

The Sponsor: The King of Wands

The Assistant or "Helper": The Page of Cups

Julie easily found some of these connections. She chose the Queen of Cups as the seated, serene woman "holding a vessel of love" to represent her wife and the Knight of Cups to represent their son, as "he's just like his other mother—full of love and always wanting to share it," Julie says. Her first cousin is male and very wealthy, so the King of Pentacles seemed a natural choice to Julie. Even though her sponsor in her 12-step program is a woman, Julie chose the King of Wands as in her deck of choice he has a deeply focused gaze.

Perhaps the more unusual associations included the Page of Pentacles as The Cheater and the Page of Swords as The Mother. A year before she did this exercise, Julie's identity was stolen. In her deck, the Page of Pentacles seems to not care much for the pentacle he's holding, reminding her of how the thief cared little about how their greed impacted her life. She chose the Page of Swords for her mother's card, as her mother died very young. Julie wasn't old enough to remember much about her mom, but her family remembered her as feisty and strong-willed, which Julie saw in the Page of Swords.

Explore this exercise for yourself. Do you have more than sixteen people you'd like to list? Do sixteen first, and then come back and do another round.[5]

Further Practice Defining Court Cards

Part One:

The Past Court

List sixteen people from your past. You may include people from the previous exercise if you wish. Drawing from further in the past rather than the recent past is preferred for this exercise, as it allows for a clearer perspective. Write a brief description of who these people were to you.

For the sake of brevity, I am only listing five of my sixteen:

1. Adam, a former boyfriend—Adam was nice person, and I was crazy about him for a time, but he was not emotionally ready for a long-term commitment. We ended our relationship because of it and I was quite sad. I'm thankful we didn't continue the relationship, as I see now that we weren't each other's best match. We averted lots of heartbreak by ending things when we did.

2. Alice, a former employer—Alice was my employer and mentor. She was steadfast, determined, and often referred to her conference room as "the war room." She was known for her astute abilities to fundraise.

3. Nora, a college friend—Nora was lots of fun, but I eventually distanced myself from her for a variety of reasons.

4. Carl, a former roommate and my first roommate post-college—He loved women (there was usually a different girl coming home with him each night) but struggled to find one who would stay with him. Despite his love for the ladies, he was never able to connect with them beyond a surface level.

5. Amanda, a former neighbor—Amanda lived across the hall from my husband and me and claimed to be happily single. She was a

correctional officer and took pride in working in what she called a "man's world."

After writing a brief description of the sixteen people from your past, pull one Court card *at random* for each of these people. Imagine that through this exercise Tarot is telling you what its Court cards symbolize by using people from your past as examples. Again, while the last exercise had you deliberately choose cards to associate cards with people, this time you will randomly pull a Court card for each person listed.

This is an exercise in which you will explore cards both right side up and reversed. Whether the card comes out right side up or in reverse, take it as a straightforward symbol of the person for whom you are pulling the card. Say, for example, you pull the Page of Wands to represent a childhood friend and the Queen of Swords reversed to represent a teacher you once had. If your childhood friend was spirited and loyal, perhaps the Page of Wands represents a spunky or loyal person. If your teacher was quite strict, the Queen of Swords in reverse might mean a particularly strict person or stringent rules. Then, make notes about what the opposite of these might be. If the Page of Wands now represents spirit and loyalty to you, in reverse it might mean lethargy or disloyalty. Likewise, an upright Queen of Swords may mean relaxed rules.. The latter definition certainly varies from more traditional meanings, but that's one of the beautiful things about self-readings—we develop our own accurate language with Tarot. Particularly if you are not familiar or comfortable with reversed cards, this will be helpful in exploring them. Examples of both are below.

Here is what the cards had to say about my list:

1. Adam: The Page of Cups—As I mentioned, Adam was a nice person, and there was certainly affection between us. But the timing was not right for a relationship. Using Adam as an example, in my readings the Page of Cups indicates willingness, kindness, potential, but perhaps poor

timing and lack of commitment. If I receive a Page of Cups in reverse, it's a sign for me to take the next step. It may also mean an unkind or unwilling person.

2. Alice: The Knight of Pentacles—Receiving the Knight of Pentacles would suggest determination, possibly some sort of battle, and maybe success in earning or raising money. These are all things I associate with Alice. If the card were to appear in reverse, it might mean a lack of energy or an omen of failure.

3. Nora: The Page of Swords reversed—Keeping in mind that I had some disappointing experiences with Nora, the Page of Swords reversed would indicate a frustrating or uncomfortable situation. Therefore, the Page of Swords upright may mean an encouraging situation, comfortable circumstances, and warm friendship.

4. Carl: The Queen of Swords reversed—Carl's love of women but inability to connect to them suggests that if I receive the Queen of Swords reversed, a desire may be true but attainment may be a problem. Thinking of Carl's difficulty with communicating, it may suggest miscommunication. With this in mind, the Queen of Swords upright might mean great connection to a desire, success, and clear communication.

5. Amanda: The King of Swords—Thinking of Amanda's independence and self-sufficiency, receiving the King of Swords in my readings may suggest an independent, self-sufficient person or the need to embody those qualities in a particular situation. It may also suggest someone who challenges the roles normally assigned to their gender or background. The King of Swords reversed may mean codependence, insecurity, and being afraid or unwilling to step outside a comfort zone.

Again, these are associations I have made for myself to use in my self-readings. Your associations may differ, but in that is the goal! Discovering your own associations is a key component to reading for yourself.

Do this exercise for the sixteen people you listed from your past.

Part Two:

The Present Court

When you have finished, remove the cards, and on a new sheet of paper list sixteen people currently in your life. As with the first exercise, make a few notes about who these people are to you. When you've finished, randomly draw a single Court card for each of these people. Make notes about what you learn about the card, as you did in the first exercise.

Below, I've included five of the list of the sixteen people currently in my life along with the corresponding Tarot cards I randomly pulled for them. Only for the sake of space have I not included all sixteen! You will want to include all sixteen while doing this exercise for yourself. Again, you are randomly pulling a Court card for each person on your list.

1. Brandon, a friend: Page of Cups—Brandon is an unusually gentle soul. He is generous, patient, and artistically inclined. Using him as an example, should I receive the Page of Cups it may mean generosity, patience, and a gentle nature as well as artistic inspiration. A reversed Page of Cups might mean cruelty or insolence, perhaps being creatively blocked.

2. Roxanne, a friend: Knight of Pentacles—Roxanne is a friendly and trustworthy person, and so I can assume that the appearance of the Knight of Pentacles means just that. As I write this, Roxanne is looking for a new job. Perhaps the Knight of Pentacles in my readings also means

new work opportunities. Reversed, it may mean someone unfriendly and not to be trusted. It may also mean a lack of opportunity or advice against changing jobs.

3. Lilah, an acquaintance: Page of Swords reversed—Lilah is trustworthy like Roxanne, but intensely private, and it's hard to tell what she is thinking. For this reason, in my readings the Page of Swords reversed may mean privacy or keeping motives quiet. Maybe the card being right side up means being more forthright. (Notice that two very different people both received the Page of Swords reversed. I will address this in the next section.)

4. Barbara, a coworker: Queen of Swords—Barbara is what some might refer to as a liberated woman. She holds a high position within the company and works on bringing dynamic ideas to the table. She challenges norms. If Barbara is the Queen of Swords, the Queen of Swords is someone, possibly a woman, who commands authority and likes to challenge "the way things have always been done." With this in mind, the Queen of Swords reversed might mean a willingness to go along with the flow and perhaps not commanding authority.

5. Tyler, a neighbor: King of Swords—Tyler is friendly and likes to strike up a conversation, but my husband and I have often heard him shouting on the phone through the very thin walls of our building. We are happily on friendly terms with the guy, but we wouldn't want to be on his bad side. The King of Swords might mean a great ally but a terrible enemy. In reverse, it might mean that someone is not such a great ally, nor much of a foreboding enemy.

Part Three:

Devising Your Court Card Character Code

In this part of the exercise, you may find that some of these Court cards literally represent individuals from your past or present. For example, if I were to pull the Page of Cups in a reading, it may specifically represent Brandon or a situation involving him. This will not always be the case. More often, the readings will reflect the associations you made in the previous exercise and not the specific individuals. In my case, the Page of Cups will be more likely to represent the generosity, patience, gentle nature, and artistic inspiration I associate with Brandon, but not specifically Brandon himself.

Review the notes you made about each of the sixteen Court cards from both Part One and Part Two. You may find some contradict others, but some will have strong parallels. There are two ways to devise your Court card character code.

First, you can look at the two people associated with each card and reflect on what they have in common. For example, I drew the King of Swords for both our former neighbor Amanda and our current neighbor, Tyler. What do they have in common? Amanda is firm but kind. Tyler is firm but brusque. They are both respected in their careers. For me, a King of Swords in my readings means a firm personality, respect, and skill in a line of work. Because the card was pulled for two neighbors, I may also see the King of Swords as a card representing a neighbor!

The other option would be to simply combine all of the traits for both persons. For my King of Swords character code, I would list powerful, potentially frightening, helpful under the right circumstances, and challenging all roles (particularly gender roles), neighborly, skilled, brusque, kind. Some of these may seem contradictory, but the different potential meanings can allow for flexible interpretations in your readings.

Try one or both approaches. All of the notes and observations will help inform you of your personal code for each of the Court cards.

Below is a selection from my performing the exercise. I chose to use all associations I compiled, but I disregarded those that seemed too extreme in their contradictions.

1. Page of Cups: Kindness and willingness from another person, but possibly someone not ready to commit fully to an idea, endeavor, or relationship. A gentle and generous soul with maybe a touch of immaturity. Someone or something that reminds me of Adam or Brandon. Artistic inspiration. *Reversed:* Someone or something is ready for the next step, even if it doesn't appear that way. May also indicate someone or something being unkind or unwilling. Maybe creative blockage.

2. Knight of Pentacles: A battle, but one of enterprise, not conflict. Determination, maybe success in earning money. Possibly a new opportunity workwise. Someone or something that reminds me of Alice or Roxanne. *Reversed:* Lethargy, failure, a bad sign for work or a project. Not a good time to seek new opportunities.

3. Queen of Swords: Respect, especially for women. Chasing desires and achieving goals. Leadership and authority, challenging the status quo. Someone or something that reminds me of strong people in my life, such as Barbara. *Reversed:* A marked disconnect; inability to achieve a goal. Someone or something that reminds me of Carl.

4. King of Swords: Independence, self-sufficiency, a situation not natural to me but one in which I can thrive, anyway. A friendly person or situation that can be harsh—a better friend than an enemy, like my neighbor, Tyler. *Reversed:* Codependence, insecurity, a sign of something not being a right fit.

As a reminder, these interpretations are mine and are meant to be teach-ing examples, not instructions for interpretation. If they help you develop your own interpretations, that's great! My students often learn from one another's interpretations. Your associations with these cards are likely to be different. My own associations are definitely not meant to trump yours.

The Sixteen Masks—Court Cards as the Roles We Play

This next exercise will explore how the Court cards can shed light on specific aspects of yourself, particularly in how you relate to others. Our selves are fluid, and our roles with others change. I recommend using this exercise to better understand the dynamics of the cards as well as to check in with yourself, perhaps as part of a yearly growth reading.

This exercise is particularly helpful in building a language with the Court cards of your Tarot deck. You may find some of the cards line up exactly with what you've discovered through previous exercises. Some may be different—even radically so. Remember, take note of it all, as you never know when even seemingly contradictory understandings of the cards will be absolutely accurate in a future reading.

For this first part of the exercise, write down your thoughts about your roles within the examples below. For example, for your role among your friends, you might write "supporter, cheerleader, group-outing organizer" or "confidant, comforter, nurturer." Some might take a little more thinking, such as describing our relationships with strangers. Strangers frequently approach me for subway directions, and so for this section I wrote "a guide." A few questions are more abstract, such as your role to authority. Maybe you challenge authority. Maybe you support it? What sort of authority role do you have, yourself?

Define your role in these relationships:

1. Friends

2. Romantic partners

3. Acquaintances

4. Strangers

5. As a parent (or godparent, aunt and/or uncle, etc.)

6. As a child—to your biological, adopted, or parental figures

7. Extended family

8. Local community

9. Neighbors

10. Legacy—ancestral or inherited patronage, such as your biological or adopted ancestors, or even the ancestors of those who did work you do now. (As a Tarot reader, all Tarot readers of the past are ancestors to you!)

11. Work—your role with those you work with through employment, volunteering, full-time child or elder care, or collaborative schoolwork if you are a student. If you are currently retired or unemployed, reflect on your role(s) when formerly employed.

12. To those in authority

13. As an authoritative figure yourself

14. In nurturing yourself—how are you kind to yourself?

15. In hindering yourself—how do hold yourself back?

16. Your health—and your role in its maintenance

After making notes about each card, remove the sixteen Court cards from your deck and shuffle them. At random, pull one Court card for each of the sixteen roles and make notes. As in the last exercise, let this exercise better help you to explore new meanings of the Tarot Court. Don't cling too hard to Court card associations you've already formed. Remember to be open to seemingly contradictory interpretations, as they will ultimately deepen your overall understanding of this facet of Tarot.

When I performed this exercise, I was unsurprised by some of the cards. I received the Queen of Cups for Card 2, my role in my romantic partnerships. I often view the Queen of Cups as a devoted partner, and my relationship with my husband is my priority. This pairing certainly made sense. I was also not surprised to receive the Page of Wands as Card 7, representing my role in my extended family. In the RWS deck, the Page of Wands seems to be a curious sort, and, looking pensively at his wand, we're not completely sure of his motivations. I often feel that my extended family sees me as someone they don't quite understand but love anyway. In my readings, the Page of Wands could be the "bohemian cousin" card!

I was surprised to receive the King of Swords as Card 8, my role in my local community. I normally consider the King of Swords to be a fierce card, but I see myself as a friendly, approachable person within my community—the lady who provides subway directions. Then again, I hold a great deal of responsibility in being a public Priestess and activist. In the last exercise, I saw the King of Swords as independent and self-sufficient, but also representing something perhaps unnatural to one's nature. Being a public presence is not something that comes naturally to me, but something I developed slowly over the years. Drawing from both of these interpretations, the King of Swords may be a sign in my readings that even something that doesn't come naturally can eventually become natural, to the benefit of myself and others. [6]

Working Outside the Binary-Gender Mold in the Court Cards

The downside to working with most traditional decks is that they usually only show two genders—male and female. This narrow view is particularly prevalent in the Court cards. Blaze, a Tarot reader, offered perspective in using these cards from a nonbinary gender identity. Blaze self-identifies as both male and female, sometimes feeling more connected to one binary gender than the other. Instead of "he" or "she," Blaze uses *person* pronouns: per/perself.

Blaze performed the previous exercise, detailed below. Blaze does not use reversed cards in per readings, so there are no potential reversed meanings in this example.

Blaze's Reading (Using the RWS Deck)

1. Friends: The Page of Wands—Blaze has a few very close friendships, and per considers friends family. For Blaze, the wand in the Page of Wands is prominent. Per noted how close to the Page's face the wand sits in the card. Blaze suggested that for perself, the Page of Wands represents intense focus and close relationships.

2. Romantic partners: The King of Pentacles—Blaze is not a fan of the King of Pentacles because of its "animal energy." Blaze is asexual and doesn't have sexual relationships with people yet would like a romantic relationship. Because of per discomfort with the King of Pentacles and overall lack of relationship experience, Blaze sees the King of Pentacles as a card of uneasiness or unfamiliarity, particularly with other people.

3. Acquaintances: The Page of Swords—Most of Blaze's acquaintances are from activist groups where they work together on common goals.

In thinking of this, Blaze sees the Page of Swords as a card of targeted action and collaboration.

4. Strangers: The Queen of Pentacles—Blaze appears as female to people who don't know per gender identity. Blaze noted that the Queen of Pentacles appears very feminine, too. For Blaze, receiving the Queen of Pentacles in per readings is a sign that things may not be what they seem and a message to pay closer attention, possibly taking more time to get to know something or someone better.

5. As a parent: The Knight of Wands—Blaze has an indirect relationship with younger people, mostly through per mother, who works with children. Blaze sometimes assists per mother, and so per relationship as a parent is more distant and impersonal, but still helpful. Noting the dry environment and distant gaze of the Knight of Wands, Blaze takes this card to mean working with or helping other people indirectly—possibly through education.

6. As a child: The Queen of Swords—"She means serious business!" Blaze said. Blaze is not in touch with per father and clashes regularly with per mother, yet their love for one another is strong. Knowing this, Blaze would expect a friendly challenge or confrontation with a loved one when receiving the Queen of Swords.

7. Extended family: The King of Cups—Blaze doesn't have much extended family. Per grandparents have passed away, and it has become very important to Blaze to know stories about them. The King of Cups reminds Blaze of per paternal grandmother, who was ornery but kind. Blaze noted something alluring about the King of Cups—per is drawn to him in the way per is drawn to per family history. For Blaze, the King of Cups represents curiosity, draw, and appeal.

8. Local Community: The Queen of Cups—Blaze felt "bland" about this card. Blaze is not sure what per role is in per community. For Blaze, the Queen of Cups might be a card of uncertainty. If Blaze received the Queen of Cups in a reading, it might signify the situation doesn't have a clear benefit, challenge, or outcome.

9. Neighbors: The Knight of Pentacles—Blaze groaned when receiving this card. "The Knight looks mean!" per said. Blaze doesn't interact with per neighbors. Blaze admitted that being neighborly is tough for per. Blaze worries about others' judgment about per lifestyle and gender identity. For Blaze, the Knight of Pentacles might be a card of criticism, especially self-criticism.

10. Legacy: The King of Swords—As mentioned, Blaze does regular activist work, but generally in a supportive role. Yet the King of Swords looked to Blaze more like an authority figure. It suggested to Blaze that perhaps per support contributes more than per realizes. For Blaze, the King of Swords may be a sign that seemingly small things may leave a lasting impact. It may also be a sign encouraging Blaze to give perself more credit.

11. Work: The Knight of Swords—While Blaze is mostly self-employed, per activism requires extensive collaboration. It is very important to Blaze that people feel safe in whatever spaces they stand in. While Blaze doesn't consider perself generally one to face things head-on, Blaze does feel it important to ride to someone else's defense when necessary. The Knight of Swords, to Blaze, is an empowering card, depicting a person who is ready to take on whatever challenge is present. Blaze sees this card as a sign to act in the name of gallantry and protection of others, even if gallantry seems scary.

12. To those in authority: The Knight of Cups—Blaze feels that a Knight's job is to go on quests and defend the kingdom, bringing back stories and riches. Per noted the difference between the Knight of Cups and the Knight of Swords. "The Knight of Swords seems more active. The Knight of Cups seems just there for show." Blaze says of per work, "I'm not there to look pretty—I'm there to get something done." But Blaze sometimes distrusts authority, feeling it's often fueled by a need to be seen. The Knight of Cups, to Blaze, is a motivational reminder to do the right thing for its own sake, and not for power or prestige.

13. As an authority figure: The Page of Pentacles—Blaze admitted that being in charge isn't per forte. The Page of Pentacles, to Blaze, seems a rather "muted" character. But Blaze felt as though per wanted to say to the character in the card, "Go do something with that pentacle. Don't just stare at it!" Through this lens, Blaze saw this card as a challenge to try something out of per comfort zone, particularly in the realm of being the authority figure.

14. In nurturing perself: The Queen of Wands—Blaze felt that the Queen of Wands looked a little standoffish and admitted that due to being shy, Blaze struggles to ask for help when needed. Per shyness might be hindering per from finding new friends, which can create loneliness. In some readings, this might mean Blaze is sabotaging perself by stepping away, but in other readings a bit of distance might be a good thing. Blaze feels easily overwhelmed by social situations but feels guilty about avoiding them. Taking both into consideration, Blaze sees the Queen of Wands as balancing the need for privacy with the periodic need to connect with others.

15. In hindering perself: The Page of Cups—Blaze found the image of the Page of Cups to be a bit mysterious. Blaze thought for a while but

couldn't come up with a specific answer as to how per might hold per-self back. Because per didn't have an answer for the question, Blaze took the card to mean a bit of mystery, particularly about perself. It may also be a card that encourages self-discovery.

16. Health: The King of Wands—Blaze likes the dignity and authority of the King of Wands. "This King isn't lording his power over anyone." Blaze felt per has a solid understanding of what's good for per health, but that there are some ways per can improve it. For Blaze, the King of Wands is a card of groundedness, but knowing there could be room for improvement.

. . .

Between the Court card character code and Sixteen Masks exercise, you now likely have a variety of personalized meanings specific to the Court cards. Moreover, these exercises will help you respond intuitively to a card, and not grasp for a previously memorized and forgotten mean-ing. I recommend trying these exercises. Keep notes and compare. Not only will it be helpful to your overall Tarot knowledge, but it also offers a glimpse in your personal journey—another of the many gifts of reading your own Tarot!

Practice with the Court Cards

You've labeled the cards with meanings from your own experiences. Now what? What do these cards mean in an actual reading? When exploring self-readings with an unfamiliar section of the deck, ask simple questions, but avoid "yes" or "no" questions initially. (For a Yes/No spread, please see page 175) Instead, pose a more action-oriented question, such as "What should I do about X issue?"

When Blaze finished the exercise above, per tried a single-card reading, pulling from the Court cards. Blaze's question was, How per could become more productive without being self-critical of perself? Blaze pulled the King of Swords. Recalling the exercise and per interpretation that the King of Swords represents small things having a large impact, Blaze took this card to mean that per is likely more productive than per realizes. Blaze's tendency to be self-critical was challenged by the King of Swords. "I'm doing okay!" Blaze said at the end of per reading.

How to Tell if the Cards Are Talking About You or Someone Else

Throughout this chapter, we've explored the varied potential for the Court cards, both as external and internal influences. But when they appear in a reading, how do we know what they're trying to tell us? Does the appearance of the Knight of Cups mean the old flame we associate with that Knight is going to call? Or does it mean there are aspects about that person we ought to embrace (or overcome) in ourselves? The nature of the question will generally shape the answer. If the question is something like, "What will happen on my vacation next week?" and the reading includes a Knight of Cups, we might meet someone who reminds us of that old flame—or that old flame has booked a ticket for the same trip! If we ask something akin to "How will travel affect me next week?" then receiving the Knight of Cups may indicate feelings or situations we've come to associate with it.

In some Tarot card spreads, it won't be so easy to tell. This is particularly true if you're working with a more traditional spread, such as the Celtic Cross (which can be found on page 218). If a Court card appears during your reading and you're unsure whether it's an internal or external influence, draw a clarifying card from the Major Arcana. This does not mean you need to separate all of the cards in the deck; merely flip through until you come across a Major Arcana card. If the first Major Arcana card is a character card, then the card in question indicates another person, or an external influence. If you pull a Major Arcana card that indicates a lesson, such as Judgment or the Wheel of Fortune, the card likely indicates feelings or internal influences. The exception to this would be the Fool. The Fool is a character card, but it will more often refer to an internal influence rather than an external one. Chart 1 on the facing page may prove to be helpful.

In this practice, paying attention to the cards' reversed or upright positions will provide even greater depth to what they may mean for you. See chart 2 on the facing page.

Recently, my card of the day was the Page of Wands reversed. Reversed cards as cards of the day are tricky for me, so I flipped through my deck until I received a Major Arcana card, which was Strength. I associate the Page of Wands with industry and creativity and Strength with potential. Receiving the Page of Wands reversed with Strength upright (a combination that can mean unfinished business, as noted above) was a message that the reading was about something going on with me. It told me that even though I was tired, I needed to push through the fatigue, complete what I had started, and finish strong.

The Cards in Action

In this exercise, we'll be working with the Major Arcana and the Court cards combined. Shuffle together the twenty-two Major Arcana and the sixteen Court cards from your deck, setting aside the numbered Minor Arcana cards. Practice with an open-ended question, avoiding yes/no questions at this time.

CHART 1

Internal Influences	External Influences
0 The Fool	1 The Magician
7 The Chariot	2 The High Priestess
8 Justice	3 The Empress
10 Wheel of Fortune	4 The Emperor
11 Strength	5 The Pope
13 Death	6 The Lovers
14 Temperance	9 The Hermit
16 The Tower	12 The Hanged Man
17 The Star	15 The Devil
18 The Moon	
19 The Sun	
20 Judgment	
21 The World	

CHART 2

Court Card	Major Arcana	Potential Meaning
Upright	External/Upright	Prominent or public ally or enemy
Upright	Internal/Upright	Self-Honesty, Agency, Ownership
Upright	External/Reversed	Loss of relationship, lack of communication. Difference of opinion.
Upright	Internal/Reversed	Unclear personal motives. Lack of direction. Caught at crossroads.
Reversed	External/Upright	Anonymous assistance or thwarting. Aid trying to reach you, or destruction trying to reach you. Disconnect.
Reversed	Internal/Upright	Personal secrets, lack of self-awareness. Personal development unfinished.
Reversed	Internal/Reversed	Disinterest, stagnation, possibly depression or physical illness.
Reversed	External/Reversed	Separation of paths, difference of opinion or morals, could be joining forces with someone also planning to go a different direction.

Colin wanted to adopt a dog from an animal shelter, but he wanted more information about how the dog would adapt to life in his home. Colin drew four cards from his combined Major Arcana and Court cards, placing them in this order: top, left, right, bottom.

Card 1: The situation in question—The Queen of Wands. Colin first noticed the woman sitting calmly with a cat at her feet. Even though the animal is a different species, he interpreted that the dog would quickly feel at home.

Card 2: Potential concerns—Judgment reversed. Colin was a little confused by Judgment reversed, so he pulled an additional card to clarify and received the King of Pentacles reversed. This suggested to Colin that he needed to make changes in his spending habits, seeing both reversed cards as a message to "overturn" some poor decisions in spending.

Card 3: Potential work—The Hermit reversed. Colin has lived alone for a while. The Hermit being reversed suggested an end to a solitary life by the inclusion of a dog, and an adjustment to his lifestyle to care for another creature.

Card 4: Guidance—The Knight of Pentacles reversed. Colin normally sees the Knight of Pentacles as taking proper time and care in making decisions. But in this case, because the card is reversed, he felt it was a message to not beleaguer the decision, as the dog he's interested in adopting could be taken home by someone else or euthanized.

Colin felt confident after his reading, as his biggest question was whether the dog would be a good fit in his home. The main card was right side up, while the others were reversed. He took this to mean that despite his concerns, the most important thing was solid: he would be comfortable and happy with his new little friend.

· · ·

Court cards are nuanced, informative, and sometimes even humorous. They serve as a bridge between the monumental Major Arcana and the more common situations depicted in the Minor Arcana. Despite this, they can still be some of the trickier cards to learn in Tarot. The biggest question that may come up in a self-reading might be, "Is this me or someone else?" Also, certain cards turning up for certain questions may incite alarm. Say you are doing a reading on your relationship and get a King of Swords when you would much rather see a Knight of Cups. Does this mean an argument is brewing? Maybe. Maybe the King of Swords is there to encourage new boundaries. Then again, maybe the argument you saw in your self-reading will only be over what type of ice cream to buy.

The nature and meanings of the Court cards are also strongly supported by the numbered cards in the Minor Arcana, known as the Pip cards. We will explore these in the next chapter.

FOUR

NUMBERED CARDS OF THE MINOR ARCANA

The Minor Arcana refers to all fifty-six cards in Tarot, aside from the twenty-two Major Arcana. The Minor Arcana includes the Court cards, but this section will focus on the forty numbered cards broken into four suits and labeled Ace (or 1) through 10. If the Major Arcana represents major passages we experience or roles we embody and the Court cards represent important individuals, influences, or "masks" in our different situations, the Minor Arcana represent different situations and choices. This does not mean that the Minor Arcana carries a smaller impact than the Major Arcana. The Minor Arcana includes the deeper nuances of our journeys, revealing the profundity of ordinary moments and simplicity of major moments.

The Suits of the Minor Arcana

As mentioned in the previous chapter, the four suits (Pentacles, Swords, Wands, and Cups) are associated with Earth, Air, Fire, and Water, respectively. These associations are known as *elementals*, which represent different facets of the human experience. An experience of the heart is considered Water, while experiences of the body are considered Earth.

Communication and conflict are connected to Air, and passion, chemistry, and sexuality are associated with Fire. In the last chapter, we explored the relationship between Cups and emotions and relationships, Swords and conflict or communication, Pentacles and wealth and the body, and Wands and passion and spirit by exploring the "rulers" of these suits, through the Kings, Queens, Knights, and Pages. In this chapter, we will explore their presence in the forty remaining Tarot cards—often called the Pips.

The Numbers

These numbered cards depict the spectrum of experience within their elemental suit. In general, as the numbers increase, so does the intensity of the experience. The card's number can also mark a point in the journey from beginning to completion. For example, the Ace of Cups may represent the beginning of a relationship. The 10 of Cups could represent the ending of a relationship or the end of a phase within it, such as a couple transitioning from casual dating into deeper commitment. The difference between the Ace and 10 of Cups might also mean the difference between tender, crush-type feelings and a serious, mature love. The numerical significance will change depending on the reader's relationship to those numbers. Perhaps you have a specific religious or spiritual tradition that finds specific numbers sacred or lucky. Maybe you personally have favorite numbers. Just as your personal relationship will influence your Court card associations, your numerical connections will influence your associations with the remaining Minor Arcana.

Remember: Tarot needs to learn your system of associations—including your associations with numbers.

Many years ago, I read for a young woman who worked as a professional math tutor. About halfway into the reading, she asked why I laid prime numbers of cards on the table. I'd unwittingly created spreads in patterns of three, five, and seven cards. The client said she had a particular fascination with prime numbers. The fact that I unintentionally pulled cards in prime amounts made her reading especially poignant.

Your relationship with numbers is important in reading your own Tarot. A dozen books may tell you that the number five is one of conflict, but if five happens to be your personal lucky number, getting a number of fives in your self-reading may be a good omen. The number nine typically has connotations of abundance, either abundant joys or sorrows. However, one of my students had a very different relationship to the number nine. She had a hard time connecting "abundant joy" to the number nine. In discussing what she thought of when reflecting on the number nine, she mentioned she was nine years old on 9/11/01. That was also the year she was sent to a foster home, where she lived for roughly nine months. For this student, the number nine signified destruction, but also survival. Understanding her personal connection with the number helped her self-readings tremendously.

If you already have a relationship with certain numbers, make note of them in your Tarot journal. For me, seven was my favorite number as a child. Receiving a seven means joy in the context of the suit in my self-readings. (The 7 of Pentacles means joy in work, for example. The 7 of Cups means joy in love or relationships.) Because of my Catholic upbringing and current work with Celtic mythos, in my readings the number three means a divine influence, as in both Catholic and Celtic Pagan lore the number three signifies the presence of the Divine. If you have associations for all numbers one through ten, that's wonderful. Use them! If you only have a few, that's fine, too. If you have no associations, don't worry! The next exercise will explore traditional numerical associations and explore ways to relate to them.

Identifying Your Keywords for the Numbered Cards

The following section contains common meanings for the numbers in the Minor Arcana as written by classic and contemporary writers on Tarot and other forms of card divination.[1]

Before reviewing those meanings, examine each of your Minor Arcana cards individually. Look at the story in the picture, *without* looking at the keywords listed below. What details in each image call loudest to you? For example, say you were looking at the 9 of Pentacles. In the RWS deck, a woman stands in a vineyard, looking at a bird on her hand. The lower left corner finds a snail. Maybe you see the character's expression as serene. Maybe you see it as bored or sad. Maybe the bird seems to be speaking a message to her, or maybe she's simply enjoying its beauty. Maybe snails creep you out, making this card a bit repulsive. Maybe you love snails and this card brings you joy. Whatever your feelings, make notes about your personal keywords in your Tarot journal.

Next, review the traditional keywords associated as listed below. Mary Greer suggests in *21 Ways to Read a Tarot Card* to review common keywords for each numbered card and pay attention to the keywords that particularly resonate for you. Make note of keywords that immediately correspond with the details you noticed when looking at the Minor Arcana cards. Also make note of keywords that make sense when you read them, even if they don't match the details you originally noticed. For example, both the keywords "attainment" and "religious rite" are used for all nines. Perhaps you did see "attainment" in the 9 of Pentacles but did not immediately see "religious rite" in it. Yet after reading "religious rite" in the Nines' keywords list, the character in the RWS 9 of Pentacles communing with a winged creature evokes religious symbolism. Another keyword for the Nines is "limits." Let's imagine that's one keyword that doesn't resonate with your impression of the 9 of Pentacles at all. If so, ignore that. Make notes of the keywords that help enhance your overall understanding of the card.

As you may notice, some of the numerical keywords may seem contradictory. Others may list similar keywords for more than one number. You may discover in your readings that a number suggests love in one context but loss in another. This is one of the beautiful, albeit sometimes frustrating, mysteries of Tarot. But just as our own languages can attribute contradictory meanings to single words or a single meaning to several words, so too can Tarot for its cards.

Following is a list of general meanings for Tarot card numbers.

The Aces

The overall sense of the suit, strength, force, authority, newness, simplicity, focus, potential, a beginning, achievement, a seed, concept, conception, nourishment, invention, contentment, extreme or excessive. *Reversed:* Delays, missed opportunities, inner focus, something of rare value, change, "false heart," confinement.

The Twos

A pair, a couple, a meeting, a choice, balance, cooperation, alliance, inner truth, partnering, response, reaction, retention, noting caution, unfolding, fortune, emotion, a message, friendship. *Reversed:* Imbalance, indecision, disharmony, opposition, duplicity, division, discord, melancholy, sadness, fear, embarrassment, obstacles, lust, lies.

The Threes

Fertility, production, the family, the Holy Trinity (or other sacred variation of three), cheer, blessing, creation, togetherness, love, integration, the result of a union, collaboration, expression, fulfillment, understanding, completion, motherhood, childbirth, understanding, passive potency, divine influence, equality, enterprise, noble causes, consideration, success, travel. *Reversed:* Uncooperative, nonworking, inaction, recovery and healing, interruption, cessation, weakness, vile action, ends, conclusion, mental worries.

The Fours

Consolidation, rest, foundation, harmonization, establishment, order, love, mercy, stubbornness, solidity, manifestation, society, association, gratification, legacy, annoyance, solitude, retreat, reliability, limiting, the Four Horsemen of the Apocalypse or Four Archangels, a difficult situation to change—either for better or worse. *Reversed:* Insecurity, rashness, inner foundation, disconnect, limitations, obstacles and delays, novelty, economy, savings.

The Fives

A cluster—of friends, enemies, blessings, or problems, frequently a number of conflict but considered Magickal in some systems, trickery, altercation, destabilization, crisis, upset, problem-solving, conflict, regrets, a union of opposites, marriage, movement, strength, wealth, accord, convenience, inheritance, loss. *Reversed:* Inertia, dogma, repression, victimizing, conformity, trickery, discussion, disorder, dissipation, loss, illness.

The Sixes

Intuition, confidence, trust, teamwork, a caution against intrusion, combination, choice, reunion, support, reciprocity, attraction, discrimination, opportunities for success, beauty, gratitude, harmony, a cycle, a union of justice and mercy, service, the present moment, witness, memories, path. *Reversed:* Self-centeredness, vanity, estrangement, self-actualization, insubordination, inferiority, misgivings, apprehensiveness, jealousy, lust, resurrection, display of love.

The Sevens

Frequently considered lucky, also considered the number of the mystic, higher knowledge or secrets revealed, misfortune, psychic attack, Magickal trouble, the "odd person out," challenges, tests, use of skill and courage, effort, possible loss of stability, victory, vice, power and energy, completion, hesitation, discussion, wealth, thought, hope. *Reversed:* Arrogance, deceit, paranoia, cowardice, implementation, uncertainly, irresolution, light-heartedness, anguish, mistrust, project, good counsel.

The Eights

Success, particularly in matters of material gain, reliability, organization, intellectuality, regeneration, resurrection, complexity, adjustment, reevaluation, organization, progress, glory, perfect balance, resolution, answering to the divine call, examination, scruples, honesty, critical position. *Reversed:* Poor judgment, lack of persistence, spiritual progress, expansiveness, interior disputes, avarice, happiness, difficulty.

The Nines

Limits, strength, prudence, attainment, completion, solitude, realization, satiation, calm, melancholy, satisfaction, completion, fulfillment, effects of previous actions, realization, victory, religious or spiritual rites, abundance—either of joy or sorrow, power, cautioning against tendencies to either enable or dominate, embracing personal power. *Reversed:* Lacking discipline or self-awareness, dependency, hostility, uncrossings, strength in opposition, deception, bad faith, vain hope, physical well-being, justified doubt.

The Tens

Wholeness, consumption, heritage, completion, the end of a chapter, a new beginning, a life shift, effects or results, permanence, renewal, community, dominion, fulfillment, divinity, androgyny, building, residency, citizenship, sorrow, a natural loss. *Reversed:* Too much of anything, rebellion, losses, quarrels, short-lived results, communion with the soul, treachery, disguise, oppression, fatality, destiny, agitation, advantage, profit.

. . .

If you are tempted to memorize these meanings, don't. First of all, it's simply not necessary. The goal is to discover your personal associations, not memorize the associations of others. Second, too much rote memorization will impede the intuitive messages necessary for accurate self-readings. However, it is helpful to have basic context for each of the cards. Refer to your Tarot journal for notes you made in the keyword exercise, which will be a resource should you find yourself stuck or confused during a reading. However, even your own notes shouldn't be a crutch. Let the traditional meanings be the pot and soil, and your interpretations the seed. Let the true meanings root, blossom, and surprise you as they unfold.

Developing Intuitive Responses with Your Cards

Your readings will be more efficient and accurate when you are comfortable enough with the cards to garner a meaning from them without referencing a book—including your Tarot journal! Associating keywords with your cards is the first step in building a contextual frame for your intuitive responses to grow.

Labeling the Cards

Our intuitive responses to the cards will change and evolve—sometimes even within a single reading. In doing the next exercise, don't draw on what you know of the card from previous readings. Focus instead on what it signifies for you at the present moment. What images particularly stand out? In recalling the elemental significance for each suit, how does that inform your understanding of the card's meaning? For example, perhaps when you receive the 7 of Swords in a reading, you generally focus on the burden the character is carrying. But perhaps today the smirk on the character's face is what's prominent. Perhaps today the card doesn't mean "burden," it means "having the last laugh." Being that the elemental correspondent of Swords in most decks is Air, ruling thoughts and communication, maybe today the 7 of Swords means freeing oneself from the burden of others' judgments.

Lately, when I've looked at these Aces in my RWS deck, I focus a lot on the hands. The disembodied hand reminds me of the pure potential of that card's suit. For me, the Ace's keyword is "absolute." I see the Ace of Cups, and I think "absolute love." For the Ace of Wands, I see "absolute creativity." For Swords and Pentacles, I see "absolute determination" and "absolute opportunity." I also get the sense that something is being offered to me, looking at the outstretched hands. If I were to receive these cards in a reading, I would take these as a message to seize an opportunity. However, when I flip the cards upside down, it looks to me as though something could be dropped. If reversed, it would mean a potentially missed opportunity or even a sign that I need to let go of something.

My friend and fellow Tarot reader, Sandra, sees the Aces as all new beginnings: new love, new work, a new project, a new way of thinking. She sees a massive amount of energy in a small unit. Sandra views the Ace as like a seed with lots of power within—a vessel to bring something greater into the world. For another reader friend, Gretchen, the Aces signify singular motivation: the big idea, the big effort, putting love out there for the first time, the first bit of money or first check.

For a long time, the Twos have embodied choice in my readings. Looking at the 2 of Wands, for example, the character gazing at the globe seems to be considering a choice. If I pull a Two in my personal readings, I often take that as a sign that a decision needs to be made. If the card comes up in reverse, it may be a sign that the time is not right to make a decision. The slight difference is the 2 of Swords. In the RWS 2 of Swords, the blindfolded woman with crossed arms suggests refusal, either refusing to compromise or refusing to make a choice at all. When I receive the 2 of Swords, I ask myself what I might be refusing to see, or if softening into a compromise might be in my best interests—or not. In my present journey I am recently married, and so the idea of "two" is evolving to mean that my choices cannot only be about one person, but must be about two people. Twos, for me, are beginning to represent a choice that impacts not only myself but others as well.

Gretchen also sees the Twos as choices, but choices related to taking first steps after the movements provided by the Aces. Gretchen uses the Thoth deck, in which the 2 of Swords shows a flower in the middle. Gretchen sees that image as choosing peace even when it's tempting to fight, while she sees the 2 of Wands as choosing to shut off distractions and focus on the work that needs to be done. Gretchen says the Twos symbolize a mirror image in her readings, and are often a sign that she will encounter an aspect of herself in another person. It's a message for her to pay attention to encounters, as they are likely to teach her something about herself.

If you are struggling to connect individual meanings with each card, look at the numbered cards as a unit.

Pull all four of one Pip set from your deck—all four Twos, or all four Threes, etc. In looking at the images, what do these four cards have in common? How do they differ? Note your first impulses when looking at these cards as a unit. Do you find the cards appealing? Do they repel you? Do you feel neutral about them? Do they remind you of anything? Make notes in your Tarot journal.

Stephanie had been reading Tarot for herself for a while, but she struggled with the numbered Minor Arcana cards. She used the Medieval Scapini deck for her practice with the Threes. When setting them side by side, she noted their stark differences. The 3 of Coins (rather than Pentacles in this deck) included a character that looked like an artist on a podium with three coins beside him depicting Venus, Caesar, and the archetypal Fool. The artist himself was on a platform, indicating some sort of reverence. To Stephanie, it seemed to represent a progression, while in the 3 of Swords Stephanie saw a family being severed. "There's a big sword that's come between the family and one character, and they look at him in disgust," she noted. In the 3 of Cups, Stephanie noted the three overly full cups, but they're "kind of icky. There's too much in them." In the 3 of Wands, Stephanie noticed three characters working together while being tied together. "It looks very industrious," she noted. "But there is some trepidation. Something about the three of them together seems out of balance."

Although the cards were very different, Stephanie could identify an argument in the 3 of Swords and Wands, while the 3 of Coins and Cups both had images that spoke to Stephanie as "gluttony and vice." Among all four cards, Stephanie found that the major theme was disharmony, mostly hidden disharmony. If Stephanie were to receive a three in a reading, she might interpret the message as disharmony, possibly covert disharmony. It may also mean that if she's dealing with personal internal disharmony, others may not be aware of it. By viewing the cards as a unit, Stephanie discovered personal meanings that are different than the standard interpretation of the Threes, but quite poignant for her.

Pairing the Minor and Major Arcana

This next exercise will help you understand your personal relationship with the Pip cards as well as practice doing a self-reading.

Pull a Major Arcana card at random. One at a time, pair each of the numbered Minor Arcana cards you are working with next to the Major Arcana card you just pulled. Practice interpreting messages from the pairs with no specific question in mind, drawing from your interpretations compiled for the numbered cards (either through the keywords exercise or the reactions to the numbered units). Knowing what you know about both the Major and Minor Arcana, what messages can you uncover when you look at them together? Some of these may answer questions you have. Others may have prescient messages to current situations you are experiencing. Stephanie performed the exercise with no questions in mind but looked for ways they might speak to current situations she was experiencing.

In a second round, select one Major Arcana card and practice pairing it with each of the four numbered Minor Arcana cards, as in the Threes, as Stephanie did.

Stephanie pulled Force, which is parallel to the RWS Strength in her deck. With Force next to the 3 of Wands, she felt the message was that if she wanted to rise to the top of a difficult situation, she would need to find strength in organization (her 3 of Wands card shows three characters climbing up a tree, which reminded Stephanie of a method of sorting something), perhaps planning her day more effectively and cooperating more with others. Force with the 3 of Cups said to Stephanie, "Put down the cake and stop drinking all the wine and go for a walk!" She saw the "icky" overflowing 3 of Cups paired with the Force card as a message for her to embody willpower over indulgence. The 3 of Coins and Force told Stephanie to employ strength to master her creative talents, possibly charging more money for her work. All three of these messages correlated to things Stephanie was personally working on and helped clarify some direction for her health, work, and personal habits. Yet, the combination of the 3 of Swords and Force still confused her.

Note: If you are having trouble gleaning a message from your pairing, drawing a clarifying card can be helpful. The clarifying card can be from either the Major or Minor Arcana.

Stephanie's interpretation of the 3 of Swords with Force was a message to employ inner strength to either walk away from a negative situation or make amends and fix it, but definitely not ignore it. Yet at first this didn't ring true for anything she was personally experiencing. She pulled another card: the Fool reversed. Stephanie felt that if the Fool were upright it would suggest that she ought to walk away and follow the Fool's message of "embracing a new path." Yet, because the card was reversed, Stephanie felt the message was to "hang in there" and not walk away. This did illuminate a current situation for Stephanie and affirmed her choice that instead of walking away she had made the right decision to stick around and work things out.

Notice the Frequency of the Numbered Cards

Pay attention to the frequency of appearance among different numbers. In my self-readings, I tend to use spreads that do not require a lot of cards. So, if I were to only pull five cards in a reading and I notice that three of them are Twos, there must be a decision I need to make, as I frequently associate the Twos with choice. The other cards in the spread can inform the nature of that decision. For example, in a recent reading I pulled three cards to represent past, present, and future. I did not have a specific question in mind. It was simply a general reading to check in with my path and influences.

At first glance, I could say this is a pretty solid reading of current and future happy times.

The Past   **The Present**   **The Future**

The Empress represents, for me, achievement in my past, as I see her as being the best me I can possibly be and making the most out of my abilities. Just prior to doing the reading, I received a potentially lucrative work opportunity. The Nines represent deep feelings: either deep satisfaction or deep insecurities. For me, these two Nines represent the former. The 9 of Cups is a confirmation that the work I'm doing is innately satisfying. The character in the middle of the card looks very happy, although there are times when I want to shake the character a bit so they don't get too comfortable and lazy! The 9 of Pentacles suggests taking things a step further, showing off their work for all to see. I took this as a message to take pride in my accomplishments, invoking the confidence of the Empress. Maybe it's a message that says, "It's okay to brag a bit, in this instance!"

What the Numbers Are Trying to Tell You

For this exercise, begin drawing cards from your deck one at a time. As you draw, separate the cards into piles. One pile will be for Major Arcana and Court cards. Create separate piles for each of the numbered cards, setting all of the Aces in one pile, the Twos in another, etc. You do not need to draw all cards. Not all Major Arcana and Court cards will end up in the former pile. Stop drawing when one of your numbered piles has all four of its numbered cards present. Set the Major Arcana/Court pile and the pile with all four of its numbered cards nearby. Place the rest of the numbered cards back in the deck. Place the four numbered cards in a row and arrange the Major Arcana and Court cards pulled around the four numbered cards. Even if you are familiar with reversals, ignore reversed cards in this exercise.

Imagine the Major Arcana and Court cards you've pulled indicate what your deck wants to tell you about the four numbered cards—through your own history, your keywords, your understanding of the unit. Look at them in the context of your numbered cards in the center. Do the presence of a few knights mean the number indicates action? Would the appearance of the Hanged Man urge restraint when the number is present? What might the Sun mean in the context of the number?

Miguel, who did not have a great deal of experience with Tarot, tried this exercise. He had to draw most of the deck to get a full Pip suit. In the end, the Tens were the first pile to have all four cards included. His pile of Major Arcana and Court cards was quite full. It included the Page, Knight, Queen, and King of Cups, plus the remaining three Queens of Pentacles, Swords, and Wands. "The Tens must have something to do with femininity or women," he said. "Maybe influences from a mother or Mother Goddess." Miguel found he'd pulled Major Arcana cards of choice, guidance, and experience. The cards that particularly stuck out for him were the Tower, the Devil, the Hanged Man, and the Wheel of Fortune. "They all seem like brick walls," he said. "A Devil only wants to get in your way, and all those people falling out of the Tower can't be a sign that things are going to continue as usual. And what good is a wheel by itself? It can't take you anywhere." For Miguel, the Tens meant endings, and ones that are kind of jarring. "But these cards look like guides," he said, pointing out that he also had the Empress, the Emperor, the High Priestess, and the Hierophant in his Major Arcana and Court pile. "It's like those other Queens—they're there to guide you."

After sitting with this exercise and these cards for a while, Miguel felt that for him, the Tens represented big things: big challenges, big endings, and big guides. He also felt a link to powerful women in the Tens, even though in his deck the Tens don't depict women. "Next time I get a Ten, I'm going to take it as a sign that something crazy may come up and try to mess with me. And if need be, I'm going to ask a woman for advice. Maybe my grandma."

Forty Mini Picture Books

One of the greatest gifts of the Minor Arcana is the breadth of story within each card. Each one could be its own reading, as each card contains a beginning, a middle, and an end. Waite even said of the Minor Arcana, "The mere numerical powers and bare words of the meanings are insufficient by themselves; but the pictures are like doors which open into unexpected chambers, or like a turn in the open road with a wide prospect beyond."[2]

To explore this, flip through your deck and remove the first Minor Arcana card you come across. Without trying to divine any prophetic message, simply take a good look at what's going on in the card. If the card contains characters, what are the characters doing? Are they cooperating or fighting? Do they seem joyful, serene, or distressed? How do the colors make you feel? Are they warm tones that invoke feelings of coziness and comfort, or oppressive heat? Are they cooler tones that suggest a chilly situation, or perhaps refreshing relief?

In the 8 of Swords, a blindfolded woman stands between a number of swords, almost like a cage. At her feet is a trickle of water. Behind her is a castle. The scene is gray. The situation seems barren, but not impossible. I gave this card to one of my students, Tynesha, who told me the following story based on its image:

> "A woman is in a challenging time. Her clothes look clean, although she's been bound and can't see anything. She may feel the swords around her but doesn't know that there's actually a separation between them. There's no vegetation on the ground, but the running water makes me think there's some not too far away. It doesn't look like she's too tightly bound. The bindings look like they're about to slip off."

Once you've determined the story of your Minor Arcana card, begin talking to the main character(s). Tell them what's going on in their situation. Be sure to mention if you see something happening to them in the future, as Tynesha did with the 8 of Swords: "You are undergoing a challenging time, but it's not as bad as you think. The situation is not as difficult as you imagine. You can slip out of the bindings and the blindfold with a little effort. Those swords around you are not a cage."

Now, take the story you've just told the characters in the card and turn it into "I" statements:

Tynesha on the 8 of Swords: "I am undergoing a challenging time, but it's not as bad as I think. The situation is not as difficult as I imagine. I can slip out of the bindings and the blindfold with a little effort. Those swords around me are not a cage."

When Tynesha told this story, she did not feel that its core message particularly applied to her. But later that week, she heard about an open position in her company (one that would have meant a promotion), and she applied for it. The process stalled as the company interviewed several other people. She wondered if perhaps she had not done well on her interview.

Frustrated, she felt there was nothing she could do and considered not pursuing the position any further. Then she recalled the message from her single-card self-reading: "I am undergoing a challenging time, but it's not as bad as I think. The situation is not as difficult as I imagine. I can slip out of the bindings and the blindfold with a little effort. Those swords around me are not a cage." Instead of giving up, she requested a meeting with her boss. During their meeting, she expressed ideas she had for the company and reiterated her interest in the position. A few weeks later, she was offered a different promotion, one that was even stronger than the position for which she'd originally applied. She suspected that tapping into her 8 of Swords message helped open a wonderful second opportunity.

Putting the Whole Deck Together

Finally! We can combine our entire Major Arcana and Minor Arcana in a reading! Shuffle your entire deck together and let's begin.

The Storyboard (A Three-Card Reading)

The following is an introductory exercise in using both the Major and Minor Arcana cards together.

Part One

Shuffle your deck and pull three cards at random. This is a simple reading, envisioning that the three cards tell a single story: beginning, middle, and end. Instead of approaching the reading with a specific question in mind, read the three cards you pulled with all of their details like a comic strip. For this first exercise, ignore reversals. Some of this will require forgetting what you've come to know about the individual cards thus far.

First, let's do a reading for a hypothetical situation. Pretend you are doing a reading for a random person on the street (not yourself). Look at the cards as though they were a storyboard for a film. What is the plot of the story? What are some of the main themes? What do you see as the biggest obstacle in the story? What lesson do you think the main character is meant to learn? Again, for this exercise, ignore any cards that come up in reverse.

Laura's Reading

"In Judgment, there's someone, maybe a judge, who's making some kind of determination. The Judge reminds me of Archangel Michael. He's going to fight for the world of the 9 of Pentacles, who is holding light and abundance. The woman in the 9 of Pentacles gets her power from the angel in the Judgment card who will fight to keep her in a place of protection and comfort. The 3 of Pentacles feels like a flashback, as though they're the ones who are telling the story of the Judgment card and the 9 of Pentacles. One character is teaching the other two about truth and power and fighting to keep both. There's something about the purple and gold in the teacher (the 3 of Pentacles) that makes me think this character carries deep insight. The others are draped in beauty, but they are not coming empty-handed. They have things to offer as well as learn. The one in orange may be a prophet in the making."

The moral of Laura's story: "There's goodness. There's richness. This goodness and richness are worth fighting for both in heaven and on Earth."

Now, try this reading for yourself with only this question in mind: *What is my current story?*

Part Two

Draw three new cards. Again, ignore reversals.

Laura's Next Reading

"I see the High Priestess as who I want to become, but if she's the start of the story, it's like I am her but am also becoming her. The cross she's wearing reminds me of how I am embracing my professorial self. [Laura is an adjunct instructor at a small college.] I'm working on the curriculum for a class I'm going to be teaching in a couple of days, and although it's been very stressful, this card twists that stress around and shows how blessed I am by this opportunity. I definitely see the High Priestess as the becoming, but there's the *am* that I'm struggling with. I am her, but I refuse to be her. If I get too much time to think about who I am instead of simply being it, I can talk myself out of doing good work.

"In the 6 of Cups, I'm reminded of both the child I was and still am, and the child I kind of wish I was. I really love this child image. (The RWS 6 of Cups shows two people, presumably children—the larger child giving a chalice to the smaller child.) I feel I identify with the little one even though I've always been the big one. The little one is getting some nurture from someone who appreciates her.

"When I see the Page of Wands, it feels like there's a journey in me. The cap he's wearing reminds me of the Judgment card in the previous reading that reminded me of Archangel Michael, who I identify with greatly. Michael destroys Satan, stamping him out beneath his feet. We all have to be conscious of the ways in which we are stamping Satan out under our feet. The wand feels natural—look at the leaves coming off it! He's a Page and not the High Priestess, which signals to me that I have greater access to what he represents within myself, just like I have access to this figure who is going to share whatever that is in the cup [referring to the 6 of Cups]. It tells me that whatever it is that I'm trying to do is far more accessible than I've let myself believe."

What is the moral of Laura's reading? "Let myself be. I struggle with being too big. I forget that I am a person who needs caring for—one who needs beauty, not only for others but also for me. My coach says to open up to the spaces of desire, but we so often disrupt these new narratives with thoughts like, 'No, you don't deserve this, you're not ready for this . . .' and we sabotage the good work that's happening for us. I feel like these three cards are telling me to work on designing a new narrative and to *be* in the grand. That feels like my natural habitat."

Part Three

Finally, do the reading with a specific question in mind. As you'll see with Anouk's reading below, you may decide to pull additional cards to help supplement the information. Pull only three cards initially, pulling more only if you find you need more. If you are comfortable with reversed cards, you will want to utilize them in this version of the reading. It is also okay to forgo reversed cards.

Anouk's Reading

Anouk has dated Erick for about six months. She's unsure whether to continue the relationship, as well as whether she should go on the trip they've planned together. First, she focused on a single question: Should I stay with Erick or end the relationship?

In the 7 of Cups, Anouk noted the dark silhouette approaching a cloud of seven cups, each with very different objects coming out of them. Some look ominous, some look abundant and hopeful, but something about all of them seems mystical, pointing out the jewels, wreath, dragon, snake. What is unknown about this card is the identity of this person. "They are totally in the dark!" she said. "The Cups are kind of revealing themselves, in a way, but there is a lot of mystery, indecision, and ambivalence. Maybe this character is overwhelmed with choice." Anouk felt the cups represented the gifts Erick brought to the relationship in the beginning: caretaking, music, intelligence, attention, even wealth. But even among all of these things, Anouk feels there is much more mystery about Erick than she feels she should have after six months together.

"A man dancing . . . maybe he's a jester?" Anouk said of the 7 of Swords. With five of the swords bundled in his arms, the character looks happy, jubilant; but he's dancing on a separate piece of land from the rest of the festival. "At first glance, the card has a joyful feeling . . . but is he stealing them? I'm not sure what this person is doing or where he's going. It doesn't even look like he belongs in the card." This card reminded Anouk of Erick and how she does not have a clear sense of his intentions in their relationship.

Anouk was drawn to the image of the woman holding a bird in the 9 of Pentacles. "I see serenity, hope, abundance, and prosperity in the environment, but there's something forlorn in her face when she's looking at the bird. It's as though something on her mind is in conflict with the bliss in the rest of this card." Anouk also thought the character might be waiting for something, which relates to her feelings of being in a holding pattern in the relationship. She did not want to give up the relationship, but the sense of comfort in the card's environment was something she was finding herself looking for outside of the relationship. Anouk saw reversed cards as a sign to pay deeper attention to the card's images. She saw this 9 of Pentacles reversed as deep concerns previously unspoken.

Anouk felt that the reading reflected and clarified some confusing feelings, but it did not answer her question of whether to stay in her relationship. She pulled a fourth card and placed it under the three.

The upside down sword, perhaps sticking into the ground, offered a very clear, immediate message to Anouk: "Stick a fork in it! It's done!" Anouk believed Tarot was telling her that the relationship had run its course. Sadly, she agreed with the message.

But there she wanted to know more. A few weeks prior to the reading, Erick had booked a vacation for the two of them on the opposite coast. Should she go, knowing that her heart was no longer in this relationship? Should she cancel, even though that would mean he would lose a lot of money? Should she wait and see what happened between the two of them in the coming weeks?

She pulled three more cards:

"This reading feels like an arc!" she said. "There's celebration, truth telling, and then a putting to bed."

The Four of Wands spoke to Anouk of a party. "The characters are likely welcoming someone, but they could also be waving good-bye." In the Moon, Anouk paid the most attention to the scorpion coming out of the water, as though "climbing onto the well-lit path, if it can get past those howling dogs."

The two cards together suggested to Anouk that something presenting itself as bright and joyful has a dangerous or unhealthy underside. Meanwhile, the King of Pentacles sits on a throne in an elaborate robe, but Anouk noticed his eyes might be closed. "He is powerful, but there's something ominous about him as well." In the reversed position, Anouk's gut reaction was that the card's message was the opposite of the image she saw in the upright King of Pentacles. Reversed, it meant a lack of power, vulnerability, and a possible loss of control. The reading suggested that going on the trip might be a bad idea, but was it possible she needed to go on the trip and see the bad idea manifest? Would that help her transition out of the relationship?

Anouk pulled two more cards.

The first was the Knight of Wands, a card she saw as swift movement and determination. "Is this a swift movement away from something, or something chasing after me, not wanting me to leave?" The final card she pulled was the Tower reversed. "People are jumping out so they don't get burned. But when it's upside down, it's acute and internal. It shows fear—my fear that wants me to hold and not act."

In Anouk's self-reading, the Knight represented momentum to do what must be done, while the Moon card suggested the clarity and honesty. "Only after truth telling and revelation can things be allowed to die and be put to bed properly." Although Anouk felt the Knight of Wands best expressed her true feelings, something still told her not to rush into a breakup. In reflecting on the Ace of Swords reversed and its "stick a fork in it" message, Anouk realized her reticence, which she previously labeled "common sense," was actually fear of change and of hurting Erick. Going on vacation with Erick would only delay the inevitable. At the conclusion of the reading, she decided to cancel the vacation and ultimately ended the relationship. While difficult, Anouk's reading confirmed that this was the right decision.

Reminders for this exercise:

♦ Pay attention to the numbers. The answer you seek may easily lie in how many of a certain number appear in your reading. Do not skip the exercises in establishing your relationship with the numbered cards.

♦ Pulling a few clarifying cards can help if a message is confusing, but don't pull too many. I recommend no more than seven additional clarifying: three for the initial reading, one clarifying card for each of the first three, and a final messenger card. Continuing to pull cards will cause further confusion. If you end up pulling seven clarifying cards and you're still not seeing the true message, take note of what your reading said, step away, and reflect on it later.

♦ If your query is a matter that is causing you great anguish, it's better to wait until you're calm before doing a self-reading. It may be there's additional information about your situation that you don't yet personally have but Tarot is still revealing. If given time, the facts will surface and make more sense.

If Your Deck Does Not Show Scenic Pictures on Its Minor Arcana Numbered Cards

Some decks do not have characters on their Minor Arcana numbered cards, displaying only literal images of their numbered suit, such as six sticks for the 6 of Wands or eight vessels of some sort for the 8 of Cups, similar to a standard deck of playing cards. If you are using such a deck, going back to the keywords exercise may be helpful. But even with the exercises, assigning keywords to cards without pictures may be difficult. Still, these decks have bountiful possibilities. If your deck does not include character images in its Minor Arcana, it may be helpful to envision a situational scale for each of your numbered Minor Arcana cards. Perhaps the Ace means "least" and the Ten means "most." Or perhaps you'd like to see the Ace as the ultimate card, and set your scale to be 2–10, followed by the Ace. Perhaps you'll assign certain situations to certain numbers. The choice is yours.

An example of the scale might look like this:

Ace through Three	Mild or Minor Situation
Cups	Small groups of friends, romance growing or waning affections depending on the question
Wands	A seed of an interest, slow stirring, some activity, growing or dwindling passion
Swords	Small conflict or problem, small changes or movements
Pentacles	Small amounts of resources, weakness
Four through Seven	Moderate Situation
Cups	Active or growing emotions or relationships
Wands	Excitement, but not overwhelming energy, possibly some collaboration
Swords	Growing but manageable conflict, abundant action or communication with more room to grow
Pentacles	Stability, potential for expansion and improvement
Eight through Ten	Severe Situation
Cups	Abundant love, a new chapter of the heart, bountiful friends
Wands	Exorbitant energy, immense power, dynamic abilities
Swords	Intense conflict or a conflict drawing to a conclusion, rapid and extreme change
Pentacles	Wealth, comfort, health, a solution to a material or physical situation

Let's say you have a question about your family's overall health. You draw five cards and get the Empress, the Queen of Wands, the 10 of Cups, the 7 of Cups, and the 9 of Swords. You will want to rely on what you know of the elemental suit and what you've assigned to each of these cards, either through keyword associations or the sliding scale. The Queen of Wands and the Empress seem to suggest more attention needs to be paid to the women in your family, perhaps those with maternal roles such as your mother, your aunts, or your grandmothers. But what kind of attention?

If you've assigned the Tens to be the strongest numbers, the 10 of Cups suggests strong intention and attention. However, the 7 of Cups, which is on a more moderate part of the scale, would suggest that some caution might be in order, maybe encouraging a limit on effusive action. The 9 of Swords is likely on the end of the scale marking severity, and the Swords themselves suggest tough situations or conversations. Perhaps this is an indication of the severity of the health situation in which the 7 of Cups will be helpful, so that communication about it does not dissolve into tears or fights.

Now let's say that you don't have a specific question in mind, but you'd like to do a reading on the events of your upcoming week. You pull four cards:

1. Overall theme of the week: 6 of Swords

2. Greatest challenge of the week: Ace of Wands

3. Greatest blessing or opportunity of the week: 2 of Cups

4. Best way to approach the events of the week: 10 of Swords

Based on this reading, we can already see that the week may involve more work than play, but that work may not make a lot of money, as there are no Pentacles at all in this reading! The Swords range from moderate to severe, but let's say in this situation that you take the Swords to mean movement and action. The moderate 6 of Swords may mean the general theme of this week is one that is a little doldrumsy. Things aren't really stuck, but they're not really moving all that much, either. The challenge is the Ace of Wands. If you take the Wands to mean power and energy, this may mean that energy could be low this week (unless you take the Ace to mean the *most* powerful, and then perhaps it's a kind of pressure-cooker energy—way too much in too small of a container!). The blessing is that there's some emotional influence available—through the 2 of Cups. The best way to approach the week, according to the 10 of Swords, may be to push through with all your might.

Practice with Reversed Numbered Cards

Reversed Minor Arcana cards provide equal opportunity for deeper inspiration as other reversed cards. As with the Major Arcana or the Court cards, a reversed numbered Minor Arcana card can indicate an internal issue, a hidden issue, a modified version of the upright card, or the opposite of the reading. As Anouk mentioned in her reading, a reversed card might be a call to pay additional attention to that card's message.

An easy method to reading a reversed Minor Arcana card is to view it through its elemental suit. Say, for example, you just went on a first date and you are curious to know if there will be any future flames with this person. Should you pull a reversed numbered Minor Arcana card, here are some potential meanings as to what it might mean:

♦ Cups reversed: Little to no potential for a relationship

♦ Wands reversed: Lacking chemistry

♦ Swords reversed: Lingering ties from the past

♦ Pentacles reversed: The relationship lacks long-term potential

If you were reading about a job you recently applied for, you might view a reversed numbered Minor Arcana card as such:

♦ Cups reversed: The job may not suit your career goals—and you may even dislike it.

- Wands reversed: The job will be dull or have few growth opportunities.

- Swords reversed: The job will lack competition, which could be positive—or boring.

- Pentacles reversed: The job does not hold much of a prosperous future.

Exploring Reversed Cards in Your Self-Readings

To further explore what reversed cards can mean for your self-readings, separate the forty numbered Minor Arcana cards and turn them upside down and shuffle, but don't riffle. Riffling would ensure that some cards would turn right side up, and for the moment we're working only with reversed cards. Set the cards aside for a moment and begin reflecting on the following situations. When you've identified an example for each of these, draw a single Minor Arcana card for each of them. Flip it in reverse and apply it to the situation.

Micheline

One of my students, Micheline, was upset with her boyfriend. He'd pressured her to quit smoking for quite some time and she finally had, but he'd not praised her achievement. She pulled the 7 of Cups reversed.

"This makes sense, because when I look at all the cups in the 7 of Cups, I see lots of attention and celebration. So if they're upside down, that celebration isn't present." For Micheline, the 7 of Cups reversed is a card of sadness, the opposite of the happiness she sees in the 7 of Cups upright.

Alex

Another of my students, Alex, worked with me privately and mentioned that their apartment had recently been infested with bedbugs. They pulled a card to represent this secret and got the Ace of Pentacles reversed.

"It's an expensive secret," Alex said. "I lost a lot of money replacing furniture and clothing. If I get this card reversed going forward, I think it's going to mean a loss that I need to keep quiet, particularly of something relating to house and home."

Myself

I drew this one for myself.

"As I'm writing this, I'm waiting to check into a hotel room. I was originally told the room would be ready in fifteen minutes, but it's now been well over an hour. It's a slight inconvenience, to be fair, but an inconvenience nonetheless."

I frequently see the 7 of Swords as burdensome and potentially overwhelming. However, in reverse it mirrors my situation. It's irritating to wait for a room when I'm under-rested and under-showered. However, I'm in a comfortable environment, and there's no real need to get into the room, immediately. I can add to my collection of interpretations that the 7 of Swords reversed is a reminder that what may feel like a big problem in the moment is probably not a huge problem at all.

. . .

This exercise will cement your own meanings to the cards, but more than that, it will open your imagination to the possibilities within each card. The link to an authentic reading is to first have a base connection with the card's generally meaning and how your contemporary situation shapes that general meaning. Both of these things are important. If you ignore your present perceptions of the card, you will remove the channel for prescient information. If you stay only with your present perception and do not take the time to learn more classic meanings, your self-readings are more likely to be confusing and formless. The combination of the two approaches allows for a flexible structure and form within the cards.

A Secret of Self-Readings

One of the frustrating things about self-readings is that they don't always make sense in the moment. This may lead us to think that we're not reading the cards correctly or that we're not able to read ourselves, period. In Tynesha's case, her interpretation was absolutely correct even if she didn't think so at the time. The situation the card mentioned simply hadn't manifested thoroughly. Don't disregard a reading simply because you aren't sure what it's referring to initially. This is where your Tarot journal will be helpful. Take notes of all of your readings, even your most cryptic ones, and reflect on them later, making note of how the situations ultimately developed. This will not only solidify your confidence in reading for yourself, it will also help continue to build the language with Tarot.

FIVE

RECOGNIZING THE VOICE OF TAROT

A fter the journey through both the Major Arcana and the Minor Arcana, we may now have a better relationship with the cards individually, but self-readings can still come with a number of hurdles. One of the biggest hurdles is doubt: *Am I only seeing what I want to see in this reading?*

If the self-reading predicts an outcome we want, we may wonder if it's only a reflection of wishful thinking. If the reading shows a scary outcome, we may wonder if (or hope) the reading reflects our personal fears and not the truth. A reflection of our feelings can certainly be helpful and validating, but sometimes we need more guidance than reflection. At this point in the book, I hope I do not sound delusional when I say Tarot will form its own opinion about the people in our lives and the choices we make. The greater challenge is unlocking that voice and separating it from our projections.

Tarot is not wholly unbiased, but it's pretty objective. Imagine Tarot as a six-hundred-year-old grandmother, leaning back in her recliner and telling you how your outfit appears to the outside world just before you head to a party. You realize the opinion has some bias. Perhaps it is tainted with a bit of old-world fashion sense. But someone who has been around for six hundred years has seen enough to be objective, and despite your own opinions, you know Ancient Grandmother speaks at least a kernel of truth. However, we may be so wrapped up in our insecurities that we only latch on to one word of criticism and ignore fifty words of compliments—or vice versa.

So, how do we hear Tarot's voice and get that (mostly) unbiased wisdom? In this chapter, we will focus on ways to break through our personal projections, open our proverbial ears, and listen to Tarot's wisdom.

Let's start with an exercise!

 ### The Breakfast Card

Shuffle your deck and reflect on the last meal you ate. Ask Tarot to describe the meal through only one card. Pull a card at random:

The last meal I ate was a small breakfast of toast topped with chunky peanut butter and a cup of tea. I associate the High Priestess as saying, "The feeling is correct." I take this to mean I made the right choice in food. My breakfast wasn't merely out of convenience or habit. I made a good, nutritious decision.

Do the same for yourself. Make notes about Tarot's opinion on the last meal you ate. Be imaginative with this exercise. It's not about "getting it right." It's about exploring the possibilities in the Tarot card.

Use the card you pulled to reflect on the following questions: Reflect on the last disagreement you had with someone. How does the card relate to the situation and, if it was resolved, its resolution? If it was not resolved, what might the card say about the potential for further resolution?

The last disagreement I had occurred two nights ago, while I was officiating a wedding. The venue coordinator was pushing the schedule and upset the bride. I first asked the coordinator to leave the room. When he didn't listen, I demanded he leave. When he finally left, I comforted the bride. Using my clergy role to diffuse the situation was, for me, a living example of the High Priestess card.

Review your previous week at work, school, or other projects or responsibilities. How might the card relate to the week's events?

I am writing this just after Samhain (Halloween). By day I work at an interfaith seminary. This past week included several discussions about Samhain's implications for my Pagan faith community. I spoke to the press a few times, sharing my personal perspective of the holiday. My faith and practices were a definite theme at work this week, so the High Priestess card makes perfect sense for me!

Banishing pushy coordinators, sharing information about a faith, and even a slice of peanut butter toast . . . all of these things feed my personal connection to the High Priestess card. Through them, I learned a little more about the card itself for my future self-readings.

With this exercise and those that follow, stretch your ideas of what you know about the cards and tap into your imagination. If you have previous ideas of what the cards mean, feel free to pull from them, but don't cling to them. The purpose of these exercises is to allow the cards the opportunity to tell you more about themselves.

Tarot's Voice Regarding the Influence of Others

In this exercise, we will be pulling cards deliberately and at random. Random pulls involve shuffling the deck and choosing a card at random. A deliberate pull involves looking at the cards face-up and purposefully choosing a card that seems to most accurately reflect the situation.

Envision a person from your distant past. With this person in mind, flip through your cards and *deliberately* select the card you feel best describes the person at the time you knew them. Then, deliberately pick a card for yourself that you feel best describes who you were at the time you knew this person.

I thought of Lana, who was my best friend from fourth through sixth grades. Lana was a sweet girl who worked diligently in school and was quite emotionally mature for her age. She sang well and excelled in school. I did not. She was very popular with the other children. I was not. I wasn't sure why she was even my friend! Because of her kind and industrious nature, I selected the Page of Pentacles—a hardworking, practical young person. This was how I viewed my friend: she was the one who did everything right, and I admired that.

For myself at that time, I chose the 10 of Wands: the person on the card fumbling to carry their load, struggling and being unable to see ahead of their challenges. That about sums up preadolescent me!

After selecting the cards that you feel best describe you and a person from your past, set the two cards aside and shuffle the rest of the deck. Ask Tarot to describe this person at the time you knew them. Pull a single card *at random*. Make notes about the differences or similarities between the card you deliberately chose and the card Tarot randomly selected. These cards represent what you imagined the situation to be and Tarot's opinion of the actual situation. Make notes about what Tarot says about you and your past person.

For Lana, I randomly pulled the 8 of Pentacles. Normally, I see this card as being equally as industrious as the Page of Pentacles, but to me it's a card more of work than of natural talent. Perhaps my friend's achievements weren't as effortless as I thought at the time. Maybe she struggled more than it showed. Yet I did choose a Pentacle suit to represent her, as did Tarot. Some of the things I felt about her, such as her grounded presence and industrious spirit, were things Tarot also picked up about her.

Do the same for the card you selected about yourself from that time period.

The card I randomly pulled for myself at that time was the 4 of Cups. The arms-crossed, closed-off character suggests love and approval is available to someone who isn't open to receiving it. Maybe that character was me, and I wasn't as unpopular as I remember. Maybe my teachers approved of me more than I knew. Maybe I was a little intimidated by my friend and didn't know how to receive accolades of my own in her shadow.

Tarot suggests that things did not come as easy for Lana as I believed they did, and I did not do as poorly academically or socially as I remember. There is no way for me to verify this unless I were to call someone I haven't spoken to in years and say, "So . . . you *weren't* a total genius?" I also don't plan to reach out to classmates I haven't spoken to since the sixth grade and say, "So . . . you *didn't* hate my eleven-year-old guts?" That would be creepy. I guess I'll just have to take Tarot's word for it!

Now let's take it a step further. Focus on a current situation that stresses or perplexes you. If you blessedly do not have that issue, focus on something that is happening to someone else. Deliberately select two cards: one to represent the situation and one to represent how you (or the person involved) feel about your position in this struggle.

Brandi used this exercise to look at a difficult work situation with a male colleague. She selected the Knight of Swords to describe the situation, as she felt the colleague was purposely sabotaging her work and she needed to be on the defensive, like the character in the card. He didn't seem to listen to her ideas, and she felt she often had to fight for recognition for her work.

For herself, Brandi chose the 6 of Pentacles, as it reminded her of a character begging for "scraps" of recognition, which paralleled her situation with this colleague.

After deliberately picking your two cards, set them aside and shuffle the remaining cards while you continue to reflect on the situation. Pull one card randomly to represent Tarot's view of the overall situation. Then randomly pull one card to represent Tarot's view of your role in the situation. Place them alongside the first two cards and compare.

Brandi pulled the Star to reflect her colleague and the 9 of Pentacles to represent herself. Her interpretation of Tarot's offerings was that this colleague saw "star" potential in her. Although his communication might suggest otherwise, his giving her more work was not meant to sabotage, but rather it suggested he might have quiet confidence in her abilities. The 9 of Pentacles suggests comfort and stability, so perhaps Brandi had an opportunity to make a positive impression on her company via the opportunities allotted to her through her colleague. Could it be possible that this colleague was more of an advocate for Brandi than she knew? Through her self-reading, Brandi decided to focus more on doing quality work than getting recognition from her colleague. If Tarot's voice was true, her work would gain sufficient recognition on its own.

Determining a Course of Action via Tarot

The question of "Am I only seeing what I want to see?" could not be more complicated than when using Tarot as a tool to divine the future. Particularly when we deeply desire a specific outcome, it can be difficult to hear Tarot's voice. As in the earlier exercise, it is helpful to practice this by first looking at a past situation.

Pick a romantic entanglement from your personal history—one that happened long enough ago. This need not be a great love. A summer camp romance or a grade-school crush will do just fine.

Deliberately select four cards to represent the following:

1. How you met.

2. How you came together. If you never ended up together, choose a card that best represents your dynamic.

3. The largest obstacle in your love story.

4. How it ended (if it ended at all).

If you cannot think of a love story, substitute a story of a friendship, a first job, or another endeavor. Whatever you choose, make sure it is far enough in your past that you can look at it neutrally—if not laugh!

My example is a brief romance I experienced in high school. I chose the following cards:

1. How we met: The 5 of Wands—I chose this because I see it as the "rowdy" card. The boy and I were part of a rambunctious group of friends. I harbored a secret crush for a long time.

2. How we came together: The 2 of Cups—The characters' positions remind me of sharing a similar secret. One day, out of the blue, the boy confessed he had a crush on me, and I confessed my crush on him.

3. The largest obstacle in our love story: The Knight of Wands—After harboring the crush for so long and finally getting what I wanted, I came on very strong—like the Knight of Wands, rushing into the situation as though on the back of a charging horse.

4. How it ended: The 9 of Swords—Like anyone with a charging horse coming at them would be, the boy got scared and broke things off. I call this image the "crying in the bathtub" card. My sixteen-year-old self was devastated and humiliated.

Next, randomly draw four more cards for the following questions:

1. What does Tarot think about the circumstances in which you met?

2. What does Tarot think about the circumstances in which you came together, if you did? (aka "the moment the sparks went off)

3. What does Tarot think about the main obstacle in your story?

4. What does Tarot think about how it ended?

Lay these cards side by side with the cards you deliberately pulled. Compare and write down your observations.

In my reading . . .

1. How Tarot views our meeting: The 6 of Wands—As I mentioned, I thought we were rowdy friends, but the Tarot chose the 6 of Wands, which shows someone on a horse riding by a crowd, seemingly seeking to get the rider's attention. Maybe I thought he and I were quite close, but perhaps

he saw me as just one of the crowd. Perhaps we weren't as close friends as I thought.

2.   How Tarot views the circumstances of our coming together: The 9 of Pentacles reversed—I chose the 2 of Cups, believing the boy and I harbored the same feelings. Tarot said we were the 9 of Pentacles reversed. The 9 of Pentacles upright shows a peaceful, fruitful garden; but when it's in reverse, the peace may not be there. Perhaps our feelings weren't quite as equal as I believed.

3.   How Tarot views the main obstacle of our story: The Knight of Cups reversed—For a long time, I believed our obstacle was the Knight of Wands—me coming on too strong, too soon. However, Tarot said the Knight of Cups reversed. I see the Knight of Cups as the archetypal romance card, but it being in reverse leads me to believe that this boy didn't really have a romantic interest, or at least he did not have the same interest that I did. Maybe I didn't wreck the whole thing. Maybe it was never meant to last very long either way. As it was a high school relationship, that rather speaks for itself!

4.   How Tarot views how it ended: The 5 of Swords reversed—I picked the 9 of Swords to reflect my sadness, plus how I blamed myself for things not working. But Tarot picked the 5 of Swords reversed. I see the 5 of Swords as a card of responsibility: one character is picking up fallen swords but leaving a few behind, perhaps for those people in the background. But it being in reverse perhaps shows that I wasn't as wholly responsible as I thought. It reiterates what the other cards indicated—this boy was never all that interested in me to begin with, so even had I been the absolutely perfect high school girlfriend, he might not have stuck around for long.

In looking at your own situation in retrospect, how does Tarot's opinion help you see things more clearly? What things does it confirm? What new things does it bring to light?

Tarot's Voice for a Current Situation

This exercise can be used for current situations, particularly those involving romance.

Marisol's relationship was at an awkward crossroads. She was familiar with Tarot but had never really practiced it. She did her own reading via the previous exercise. These are the cards she selected:

1. How Marisol met her boyfriend, Rafa: The 10 of Pentacles—Marisol chose the 10 of Pentacles because the two people in the background reminded her of the random variables that allowed her to meet Rafa. It was an unlikely meeting. They could have easily passed each other by. She felt the Pentacles represented stars aligning.

2. How Marisol and Rafa came together: The 3 of Cups—Marisol chose the 3 of Cups because she believes "there are three entities in a relationship: two people and the third, ethereal body when people enter that space." When they both felt that third, ethereal presence, they stopped dating other people and focused only on one another.

3. The largest obstacle in their love story: The 10 of Wands—Marisol chose the 10 of Wands, as she felt the character blindly walking with an armful of sticks, unable to see the beautiful village in the future, was indicative of the difficult time they both had setting down emotional baggage from previous heartbreak. It seemed to be blinding them from moving forward. Because this is a reading about a present situation, the fourth card will not focus on the conclusion (as the previous reading did), but will focus on the next steps to take in order for a positive outcome.

4. Best course of action: The 2 of Swords—Marisol felt the future for her and Rafa was unclear. Moving forward, in her mind, was a leap of faith. The blindfolded woman in the 2 of Swords appeared somewhat peaceful to Marisol, although she is not in control of the situation. This resonated with Marisol, who said she felt calm about where things were going, even though the outcome was unclear.

After deliberately choosing the first four cards, Marisol shuffled the remainder of the deck, meditating on the questions posed in the first four cards to invoke Tarot's voice. The random cards she pulled are shown on page 156:

1. How Tarot views Marisol and Rafa's meeting: The Queen of Pentacles—Tarot's choice of the Queen of Pentacles showed a woman holding the world in her hands. Marisol noted the lively, abundant image also carried a bit of sadness, though. Perhaps her meeting Rafa wasn't as random as she thought. Perhaps she carried more draw than she realized and attracted him to her.

2. How Tarot views the circumstances of their coming together: The King of Swords—This card resonated with Marisol as powerful, decisive, and determined. While she initially felt the decision to enter the relationship was mutual, Tarot's voice suggested the "third body" might be societal

pressure to "choose someone now," due to both her and Rafa's ages. It had not occurred to her until the reading that this might cause ongoing stress in their relationship.

3. How Tarot views the main obstacle of their story: The 5 of Pentacles— Marisol felt the 5 of Pentacles showed disease and an air of being forlorn and lost—but that there was also brightness to the card. It suggested a spirit of Faith. She noted how the characters in the 5 of Pentacles had a clearer view of their path, even if the snowy weather was worse for travel. She felt hopeful. Perhaps their relationship obstacles were not as difficult as she thought they might be.

4. How Tarot views the best course of action: The 9 of Swords—The similar images of the blindfolded woman in both the card Marisol chose for herself and the one Tarot assigned to the situation show a sense of struggle to find a way even though she can't see where she's going. Tarot seemed to agree with Marisol that she had pretty much done all

she could to better the relationship, and now its future course was for the Universe to decide.

Marisol felt the overarching message from the voice of Tarot's reading was that if she and Rafa were not careful, something with great potential for love could be lost. Because the cards Tarot chose were so very similar to the ones she chose herself, this reading served as a confirmation that she had a clear perspective of what was going on in the relationship.

Reading for the Future of a Situation

Neo received an invitation to teach his yoga classes at a community center near his home. He was curious to know if the clientele and management would be open to him and his work. Was taking this opportunity a good idea? Would it serve his business? What would be the outcome of Neo teaching yoga at the community center?

Neo's Selections

First, he deliberately chose one card to represent the space in question.

Neo chose the Moon to represent the space because he associates the card as one of creativity, happenings, and occurrences, but also surprises. "It's the 'Who knows what will happen?' card," he said.

Next, he chose the Wheel of Fortune to represent his greatest hopes for this opportunity.

Neo hoped this opportunity would broaden his network and build his mailing list, leading to more teaching opportunities in other places. He chose the Wheel of Fortune, as he associates this card with luck, serendipity, and connection.

Third, he chose the 5 of Pentacles to represent his greatest fears about this opportunity.

"I fear it wasting my time!" Neo said. It takes a lot of energy to plan a yoga curriculum, and he didn't want his efforts to be "dead in the water." He chose the 5 of Pentacles because he feels the card indicates poverty, being out in the cold, and a lack of connection.

A note: when using this exercise for more prophetic readings, be sure to consider your own expectations. These will likely be different from your hopes and fears. We may hope for more than we expect. We may have less fear when we actually sit with our true expectations.

Fourth, Neo chose the Knight of Pentacles to represent his honest expectations about the success of this venture.

Neo's approach to yoga is more spiritual than athletic. The slow, determined pose of the Knight of Pentacles spoke to Neo because he felt he struggled to be both a guru and a businessman. "There's a 'stuckness' I'm still working through," he added. He also mentioned he'd had a little bad luck in the previous year in terms of attracting people to his classes. Would teaching at the community center truly help him pay his bills? Neo chose the Knight of Pentacles to represent his hopes that it would.

What does Tarot think of Neo's situation?

Tarot's Selections

The Community Center

Neo was pleased with Tarot's choice of the Page of Pentacles. It made him think of offers and money. "Take it because it's there!" he said.

The Greatest Opportunity

"This is kind of weird . . . the 2 of Pentacles reminds me of a vision I had when scrying[1] with St. Cyprian.[2] In the vision, I was shown a woman in posh attire inviting me to a ballroom where my fiancé and I were going to attend a dance. I was not ready to dance. This reminds me of not being prepared. This space will be a good place to get prepared . . . to get my steps right."

Potential Difficulty

Neo pulled the High Priestess and saw it as the person who runs the center. He again recalled from his vision that the posh woman who had invited him and his fiancé into the ballroom had a forked tongue and could not be trusted. "This card tells me to beware," he said. "Not everyone I will be working with at the center will have my best interest at heart."

Neo's Overall Experience

"This is going to change everything," Neo said. "In my business, in my relationship, everything in my life, everything in my self. There was a before this, and there will be an after to this."

Because the Death card is loud and profound but also rather cryptic, Neo pulled a clarifying card to try to find out more about these changes.

Clarifying Card

The Tower indicated to Neo that this venture would be a very big turning point for him, perhaps too big to see it all at once. "Who would have thought teaching yoga at a community center would turn everything upside down?"

Neo pulled one more card to sum up the reading: What would best serve him? What action should he take for the greatest potential and well-being? He received the 6 of Swords.

"I need to move slyly and carefully, in a well-prepared manner," he said. "This will be a much bigger adventure than I initially thought."

• • •

Notes About Using This Exercise

Marisol and Neo asked simple, direct questions about their situations and built readings to suit what they needed. When you approach Tarot with your questions, be straight, direct, and honest about what kind of information you need. Are you examining your hopes? Your fears? Your honest expectations? Be sure to include a card for each of the angles you wish to see, but don't pull too many cards. You can find yourself in a confusing, questioning loop. The ideal number of cards for this exercise is eight: four single cards deliberately pulled for 1) the situation, 2) your hopes, 3) your fears, and 4) your honest expectation about the outcome; then four at random to find Tarot's perspective. If you need a couple of clarifying cards, pull no more than two. Set an absolute limit of ten cards for the reading, but pull as few as you are able. Each card has an infinite number of messages for you within it. Don't overwhelm yourself by pulling too many.

It won't always be necessary to deliberately select cards. With enough practice, you will pull randomly from the deck and still hear Tarot's voice. The exercise can be very helpful when first reading your own cards, particularly when the situation is one in which you're heavily invested and are struggling to see an outcome.

Unlocking the Voice of Your Deck

I haven't counted in a while, but I think I have nearly twenty decks. While I can use any one of them to divine a specific question, I have found that some of my decks prefer one topic to another. I have one deck that is very good with love readings and another that is great with career questions. The exercise below is meant to help determine your deck's preferred topics and when it's best to use it.

First, shuffle your deck with no specific question in mind. Focus less on intention for this reading and more on the feel of the cards in your hands. Then randomly pull a single card. This first card will tell you what your deck wishes you to know about it. Take this card as a snapshot of your deck's personality.

My student, Taylor, tried this with his deck and received the Magician reversed.

"He's pointing and saying, 'This thing? Right here? You need to work with us, all the time,'" Taylor said. Indeed, the Magician seemed to be pointing at the rest of the deck, which sat beside the card. Taylor felt this was a particularly hardworking deck that wanted to be consulted frequently.

Make notes about your initial impressions. Reflect on what you've already discovered about Tarot. If you're not sure, simply write down which card you pulled and move on to the next part of the exercise. Set the first card aside and shuffle the deck again. This time, you will ask your deck about what is best to consult it for. While a good deck can be consulted for anything, some decks will have a specialty topic. Ask Tarot what that specialty might be as you shuffle and randomly draw another single card.

For this part of the exercise, Taylor pulled the King of Wands.

Judging from the character's far-reaching gaze, Taylor said, "This deck is about perspective—it will help me look beyond my realm and show me situations over which I may or may not have control."

Notice where the cards' characters are pointing and looking. If a character is looking at your phone or computer, maybe the deck wishes to help you with communication or research. Take liberties with what questions you ask the deck about itself. If the deck were a person sitting beside you, what might you like to know about it?

Next, Taylor wanted to know how best to pose questions to the deck. Taylor pulled the 10 of Swords reversed.

"Gravity is not this guy's friend," Taylor said of the card, noting that in reverse it appeared a worse position for the character than if the card were right side up. The swords would likely dig further into the character's back while reversed. He took this to mean that the deck wants him to ask simple questions so as not to "get too complicated or weighed down" in the asking process.

Taylor then wanted to know what time of day would be best to consult the deck. Taylor pulled the Queen of Wands.

Noting that this is the consort to the King of Wands, Taylor felt the Queen of Wands meant the deck could be used at any time, for any situation.

Taylor noted that lots of Wands came out in this exercise. The fiery and passionate nature of the Wands suit suggested that this deck really loved to be used.

If you're not sure initially, simply write down what you pulled and do the exercise again on another date. Over time, compare your notes on what Tarot has said about itself. Even if the cards seem contradictory at first glance, look for where they have similarities. In addition, the deck's voice may change and develop over time.

Be mindful that your own deck's preferences will likely differ from other copies of the same deck. It will ask of others very different things from different people. Say both you and your best friend use the RWS deck. Your copy may only want you to work with it during times of trouble. Your friend's copy may only want to be a tool of self-reflection and not a problem solver. Neither is incorrect, both are accurate. Just as two mirrors may be constructed identically but will never give two different people the same reflection, Tarot is a reflection of our personal spirits, and even identical decks will reflect different messages.

SIX

REVERSED CARDS

Reversals remain one of the key areas of confusion when reading Tarot, particularly when reading for oneself. Reversed cards can provide a lot of depth in a reading. They encourage us to look at things from a different perspective and help keep us from getting into a rut with our Tarot cards. Yet, they're not always easy to decipher. I am personally a big fan of including reversed cards in my readings, but sometimes I get stuck on them, too! We've dabbled with reversed cards, but in this chapter we will dig in and really try to understand them.

The first thing to note: you do not have to read reversed cards. I know many fine readers who do not pay attention to reversals. I also know deck designers who do not consider reversed meanings when creating their decks and suggest their decks only be used upright. When I'm tired or struggling to make sense of a reading's message, I sometimes forgo the reversed cards. I encourage new readers to try incorporating reversed cards into their readings. If after working with them for a time the reversed cards still do not speak to them, perhaps reversals are simply not part of their personal reading system.

If your deck's Minor Arcana does not have illustrated characters on them, reading reversed cards may be even more difficult. For readers who own such decks, my suggestion would be to devise a personal system of meanings that may be different from the suggestions below or ignore reversals altogether when using said deck.

Potential Ways to Interpret Reversals

If you decide to incorporate reversals into your readings, here are some potential meanings to consider:

- ♦ The reversal is the opposite of the upright card.

- ♦ The reversal indicates a loss.

- ♦ The reversal is a diminished form of the standard position.

- ♦ The reversal indicates something is hidden.

- ♦ The reversal indicates a stalled situation.

- ♦ The reversal warrants special attention.

Let's take a look at each of these potential scenarios.

♦ The Reversal Is the Opposite of the Upright Card

In general, reversals most often indicate the opposite of the upright card's meaning. By identifying what you know about the meaning of the upright card, simply finding the inverse of that may reveal what the reversed card is trying to say. Let's look at a few examples.

I see the Queen of Swords as a person, typically a feminine person, in a position of power and authority. I also see this character as someone who can be very harsh, particularly with words (thinking of Swords in relation to air and communication). The opposite of this depiction would be someone without power and authority. A reversal might indicate weakness. It also might indicate gentle words.

The High Priestess is a card I generally associate with intuition. When it appears in one of my self-readings, I take it as a sign to trust my initial instincts. It is also a sign for me that Magick and spiritual work are afoot. Therefore, when the High Priestess is reversed, it is a sign that my initial feelings may not allow me to see the truth of a matter. It may mean I am cut off from my intuitive impulses. It can also represent soul loss or being detached from work of a spiritual or Magickal nature.

I see the Lovers as a card of intimacy and joy as well as connection. I also take it to mean romance or platonic love. When it is reversed, I see it as a loss of connection or a diminishing of chemistry. It may also mean some love is lost. Something I once had great affection for may be diminishing.

◆ The Reversal Indicates a Loss

Reversals can also indicate a loss, either already experienced or one soon to occur. Let's look at a few examples.

The 6 of Wands shows a person riding a horse triumphantly through a crowd. If the 6 of Wands means triumph and going places, perhaps the card being in reverse represents a loss of respect from others, possibly losing favor or credibility. In the upright position, the rider seems firm in their direction. In reverse, it could also indicate a loss of direction.

When I see the overflowing cup turned upside down, I imagine that all the water is flowing out. If water represents love and emotions and the Ace of Cups is the epitome of that, then in reverse the card may represent a loss of love. But if we consider the cup to be a vessel that contains love, the reversed position may mean a loss of emotional control.

This exercise becomes even more interesting when looking at the reversal of a card that already means loss. In the 5 of Cups, I see the cloaked figure with the hanging head and the spilled cups around them as an embodiment of loss. So what does this mean when this card is in reverse? A *loss* of loss? Quite a riddle, but perhaps this is a sign that something lost will soon be found or a perceived loss is not actually a loss at all.

◆ *The Reversal Is a Diminished Form of the Standard Position*

If we imagine that each card is a song, when the card appears in the reversed position, it's singing the same tune but the volume is turned down. The meaning is the same, but the situation does not carry the same level of urgency.

The Knight of Swords may mean battle, travel, or a war of words. In any Knight card there is a call to action. Of all the Knights, the Knight of Swords is the most extreme. In the RWS deck, this Knight appears to move the fastest out of all four. When it's reversed, this may be a sign that the situation in question does not warrant immediacy. Action may be required, but not yet.

If the King of Cups represents strong love and commitment, the reversed position of this card may mean love is present but not overwhelmingly so. Commitment may also be present, but the depth of the commitment may not be as strong as if the card were upright. The King of Cups is also known to mean benevolence or kindness. Perhaps when reversed it represents kindness without overt effusion.

The Hanged Man is the ultimate "stuck" card. When reversed, it may mean a delay, but not a major holdup. The Hanged Man in reverse can also mean something previously stalled is suddenly free, and it suggests great movement when previously there was none. Honestly, this is one of the best cards that I can personally see getting in reverse!

◆ The Reversal Indicates Something Is Hidden

Some reversals carry the same meanings as their upright cards, but they indicate that the situation in question is a secret.

In the Wheel of Fortune reversed, a major change is coming but no one knows about it. One example of such a reversed card would be an elopement!

The 4 of Cups is a great messenger card. In this depiction, a cup appears out of thin air and is being handed to a person sitting under a tree who perhaps didn't expect the message. Receiving this card in reverse might mean hearing or keeping a secret.

The 10 of Pentacles commonly means health or money, and an abundance of it! When it's in reverse, it may be a sign to keep your money close or to not reveal all of your strengths right away. The reading may be cautioning you about sharing resources and encouraging you to keep them to yourself.

♦ The Reversal Indicates a Stalled Situation

A reversal may also indicate a stall in whatever situation the card embodies. This is particularly true for cards that typically indicate movement, such as the Wheel of Fortune, the Chariot, any of the Knights, etc.

The RWS deck 3 of Pentacles shows two people approaching someone with a document, possibly with plans in mind. Therefore, plans may be on hold if one were to receive the 3 of Pentacles in reverse.

The 10 of Wands can suggest stalling when it's upright. In reverse, this might mean that an intended pause or constructive break might be delayed itself.

If the Queen of Pentacles is a card of production, reproduction, or a sort of bountiful endeavor, receiving the card in reverse may mean a serious delay.

Some readers take a reversed card to mean that special attention needs to be paid to it, likening it to a red flag in the reading. This is particularly true if you only have one or two reversed cards in a larger spread. Hannah received the Page of Cups, the Chariot, the Hierophant, all upright, and the 7 of Cups reversed. The first three cards related to her impending separation from her partner, which was amicable, as confirmed by the Page of Cups, a card she sees as kindness. The switch in her life was one she needed for her personal autonomy, which was reflected by the Chariot and the Hierophant. The fourth card she pulled was meant to depict what she wouldn't expect. She pulled the 7 of Cups reversed. The plethora of cups in the card suggested that despite the fact that she and her partner were parting on positive terms, she would still need to pay close attention to the feelings of others—both of her partner and other people in their lives.

How Do I Know Which Reversal It's Supposed to Be?

You've read through all possible reversed meanings and thought about them in relation to the cards, but when a card is drawn in reverse, how do you know which reversal it's supposed to be? Is it the opposite, or is it a secret? Is it a modified version of the upright card, or is it a red flag? As you become more acquainted with self-readings, this will become apparent, as your intuition and language with Tarot grows. But while that relationship is developing, the exercises below may help.

In chapter 3, we practiced determining whether a Court card is an aspect of personality or a role one is playing in the broader world. This similar exercise uses the Major Arcana to clue us into what a reversed card may mean. If you pull a reversed card and need to know which of the above categories it likely means, flip through your deck until you receive a Major Arcana card. The chart below can provide a clue as to what the reversed card may be trying to say.

Major Arcana Clarifying Card	Reversal Meaning
0 The Fool	The opposite of the upright meaning
1 The Magician	The opposite of the upright meaning
2 The High Priestess	Something hidden
3 The Empress	A diminished form of upright meaning
4 The Emperor	A diminished form of upright meaning
5 The Hierophant	Pay closer attention to reversed card
6 The Lovers	The opposite of the upright meaning
7 The Chariot	A stall
8 Strength	Pay closer attention to reversed card
9 The Hermit	Something hidden
10 The Wheel of Fortune	A stall
11 Justice	Pay closer attention to reversed card
12 The Hanged Man	A stall
13 Death	A loss
14 Temperance	A diminished form of upright meaning
15 The Devil	The opposite of upright meaning
16 The Tower	A loss
17 The Star	Pay closer attention to reversed card
18 The Moon	A diminished form of upright meaning
19 The Sun	Something hidden
20 Judgment	A loss
21 The World	A loss

Melanie accepted a job teaching poetry at a community college near her home. When she asked Tarot what challenges she might expect, she pulled the 8 of Cups reversed in a single-card reading.

Not knowing what that meant, she flipped through her deck until the first Major Arcana card appeared: Justice.

Using the chart above, Justice suggested to Melanie that she might want to pay closer attention to the meaning of the 8 of Cups. This is a card Melanie associates with "the hurt person," noting that they are wandering off alone, as though they've been turned away or their feelings were injured or neglected. "I may have some very sensitive students in the class," she said when she looked at Justice and the 8 of Cups together.

Yes or No Questions

One of the most convenient ways to include reversals in your reading is through a yes or no question. This simple formula has worked for many of my students over the years. Not only does it provide a clear answer, but the content of the cards provides further information with regards to *why* it's a yes/no answer.[1]

◆ *Three Cards Upright: Strong Yes*

Anne wanted to know if she would travel more in the coming year. The cards she received were all upright: Strength, the 10 of Wands, and Temperance. Travel was definitely in her future. Strength suggested to Anne that her plans were in good order, but the 10 of Wands made her think that perhaps there would be more effort in making the travel happen than she initially thought. Temperance suggested that she may want to scale back a bit on her plans or trim the budget in other areas of her daily life in order to make travel even easier on herself.

◆ *Two Upright, One Reversed: A Qualified Yes (aka "Yes, but . . .")*

Rick was approaching his fiftieth birthday and wanted to know if he will enjoy his milestone year. He pulled the Knight of Wands, the 3 of Cups, and the 5 of Pentacles reversed. The answer was yes—the Knight of Wands and the 3 of Cups both symbolize happiness and joy to Rick. But the 5 of Pentacles reversed suggested a caution against overextending energy and money. Happiness may be better found through conservation of fiscal and personal resources. "Tarot wants me to tone it down a bit," said Rick. "I'm okay with that."

◆ *One Upright, Two Reversed: Unlikely, but Not Impossible*

Julia was thinking of expanding her business and wanted to know if doing so would be fruitful. Her cards were the Queen of Cups reversed, the Queen of

Wands reversed, and the King of Swords. The two cards indicating powerful women were both reversed, which seemed like a doubtful answer in Julia's mind. The upright King of Swords suggested to her that in order to make this path truly fruitful, she would need to take a more aggressive approach in business. The yes she wanted would have to be fought for and won.

◆ Three Reversed: Strong No

 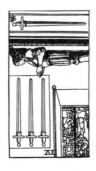 

Jeff was considering going back to school. All three cards were reversed: the Page of Cups, the 4 of Swords, and the High Priestess. The Page of Cups and the High Priestess were cards that spoke to Jeff of desire. He saw the 4 of Swords as a resting card. If the three cards in reverse meant a definitive "No, don't go," Jeff needed to reflect on his actual desires. Would school *really* help Jeff get the kind of job and/or life that he wanted? The cards said no, but they encouraged Jeff to think deeper about what he was actually hoping to achieve in school. A better paying job? A different career path? Simply breaking monotony? Tarot encouraged Jeff to ask himself these questions and see if school would answer them, or if a less expensive and time-consuming endeavor would do the trick.

If the Majority of Cards in a Reading Are Reversed

Pay attention to how many cards come out reversed, particularly if you are using a larger spread.

If the majority of the cards are reversed, it's possible that *all* cards should be flipped—making the reversals upright and vice versa. To determine if this is what you ought to do, pull one more card from the deck with this question in mind: Do I flip or do I leave them? If the card appears upright, it is a sign to flip the position of all cards in the spread. If the card appears reversed, it is a sign to leave all cards as they were dealt.

A reading with mostly reversed cards can indicate being stuck in a rut and wanting major changes. Imagine that all the reversed cards indicate areas in which things are stuck. Readings with *all* cards in reverse may mean that life changes, potentially *major* life changes, are necessary.

Miranda, who had recently become pregnant, did this Celtic Cross spread (see facing page) for herself regarding the next few months of her pregnancy. For instructions on how to use The Celtic Cross spread, please see page 208.

(In the Celtic Cross spread, the sixth card crossing card the first does not have a reversed position and should always be considered upright.)

In Miranda's reading, seven of the ten cards in this spread were in reverse. This is Miranda's second pregnancy, and she admitted that the fatigue she was experiencing was far worse than in her first. The predominance of the reversed cards suggested to Miranda that something in her life would need to change if she wanted to experience the upright Empress card at the end of the reading, which she took to mean a healthy delivery. What would need to change? The Judgment card spoke to Miranda as "exercising better judgment over my health choices and also what tasks I take on." The Star reversed suggested that some of Miranda's personal endeavors may need to be put on hold while she focused on self-care.

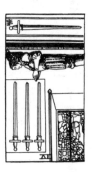

The Celtic Cross Spread

The 7 and 10 of Pentacles and the 8 of Swords, all reversed, spoke to Miranda of making food choices better aligned with her health and less about convenience, even if the convenient option may be more appealing with a toddler running around!

In Miranda's reading, and in the case of many readings in which the majority of the cards are reversed, it may be helpful to look at general themes rather than trying to interpret every reversed card. In her reading, Miranda focused on what cards particularly stood out to her and through them found what changes she needed to make. This tactic is particularly helpful when doing a reading containing mostly reversed cards.

Where Are the Characters Pointing?

If your reversed card messages aren't clear immediately, take some time to look at where the characters are pointing. The following is a reading I did for myself using the Checking In: Four Quarters Spread on page 181, without any specific question in mind. Instructions for using this spread can be found on pages 223–225.

This is quite a textured reading, which I can pull a lot of things from. I generally see the Knight of Wands as a card of energy. When it is in reverse, I recognize fatigue. Today this is quite true, as I got up very early this morning after having gone to bed very late last night! However, I am also paying attention to where the Knight of Wands is pointing. He is directing the wand at the Empress, below. For me, that is a sign to call my mother today. We've been playing phone tag for nearly a week!

A Sign to Look at Things in a Different Way

A reversed card may be a suggestion to look at things in a new way. For me, I find that cards in which another character is "looking back" at the main

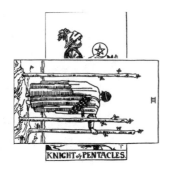

Four Quarters Spread

character in a card suggest opening my mind to another viewpoint. Some examples of cards with this sort of imagery include the following:

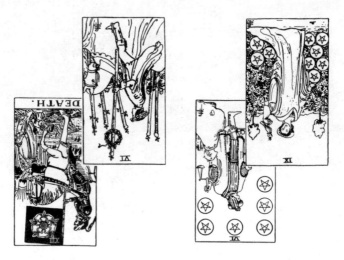

In this practice, the reversed cards open doors for increased reflection and consideration. They make us ask tough questions about who we are and what we are trying to do.

In the 6 of Wands, the horse is looking back at its rider. In the 9 of Pentacles, the bird is looking back at the lady. In the Death card, the holy man is pleading with the Grim Reaper, and in the 6 of Pentacles, an impoverished person is looking up at a benefactor. For me, these "looking-back" characters are far more prominent when the cards are reversed. They encourage me to look at the situation from a different perspective. In the 6 of Wands, the crowd is cheering for the champion, but when it's in reverse, could it mean that the champion doesn't feel worthy of the cheers? Could it mean that not everyone shares the enthusiasm? In the 9 of Pentacles, the woman is surrounded by comfort, which seems to be a blessing. But when in reverse could that blessing be more of a burden? Does she feel she hasn't earned it? Is she held hostage by an expensive lifestyle? In Death, could the loss actually be a blessing of its own? Maybe someone suffering from serious, painful illness has finally crossed over. Maybe an exhausting relationship has finally found its natural end. In the 6 of Pentacles, is charity easier to give and tougher to receive? The last card poses the question: are my acts of goodwill benefitting others or my own ego?

This practice is especially helpful if you are doing single "card of the day" readings and get a reversed card.

As You Work with Reversals . . .

As in all aspects of Tarot, reversals take practice. In some cases, they may take longer to learn than other parts of Tarot. My suggestion is to try each of the above exercises individually. Make notes of which exercises carry the most significance for you as well as which do not. In time, you'll find that some of these practices naturally apply to most of your readings, and others might never apply. You may find other reversed interpretations not even mentioned here! Don't limit yourself. Some Tarot readers I know believe there is never an end to the potential meanings in a single reading, or even a single card! Also, allow yourself to be wrong. When we allow ourselves to be wrong periodically, we leave space to build stronger relationships with Tarot. We can start to sense the minute but tangible difference between when we are looking for our choice outcomes in the reading rather than letting our intuition speak to us.

Keep reading, keep practicing. Take a break when reversals are simply too frustrating or confusing in a specific reading. Return to them later, or if you decide they're simply not for you, abandon them altogether. Remember, this is about building your language with Tarot, and whether or not you choose to use reversals and *how* you choose to use reversals is indelibly important to your self-reading process.

SEVEN

OTHER TOOLS: WHAT'S MISSING FROM YOUR TAROT READING?

PLUS HOW TO INTERPRET TOUGHER CARDS

Tarot is layered. Readings are nuanced. Many manuals on Tarot instruction, including this one up until now, focus primarily on deciphering card meanings. Yet a reading is deeper than simply the sum of the cards' meanings. This chapter examines aspects of a Tarot reading that might not be obvious immediately but can enrich your reading nevertheless.

What's Missing from Your Tarot Reading?

I first learned of this concept through Tarot reader Hilary Parry's blog post on Theresa Reed's *The Tarot Lady* blog in June of 2011 entitled, "What the Cards Are Saying when They Aren't There." [1] Hilary wrote about the practice in the context of reading for others, but the same is true in self-readings:

> If [the question is] about love, and there are no Cups in the reading . . . well, there are a couple of things that could be interpreted from that, but not limited to just these interpretations (in general)

1. a frivolous crush that isn't substantial enough to constitute a true emotional connection . . . romantic intentions might be best suited elsewhere or a focus inward is in order; or

2. the object of the . . . affections isn't interested (again, keeping in mind this is a hypothetical)

Still talking about a potential love interest, what if there ARE Cups present, but no Pentacles (Coins)? This might indicate lots of emotion, but little stability, if any. There may be lots of love but perhaps not enough of the practical aspects that go into making a relationship work.

Other helpful questions to ask yourself during your reading include: do you see lots of Cups and Pentacles, but no Wands? Maybe the love and stability are present, but chemistry is lacking. If there are no Swords, are there aspects of communication or healthy conflict missing, making things a little uninteresting or surfacey? If there are no Major Arcana cards present, it might be prudent to ask if this relationship is truly serious.

Naturally, the perfect reading would include a balance of all four Minor Arcana cards and desirable Major Arcana cards. Usually, this won't happen. However, a reading with missing elements does not automatically mean there is a fundamental problem with the situation in question. Sometimes, absent suits or pertinent Major cards reveal to us where something has room to grow:

♦ If you are missing Cups—The situation may have a dearth of love, kindness, personal investment, or heart.

♦ If you are missing Pentacles—The situation may be unstable. It may also indicate unemployment, poverty, or missing material goods.

♦ If you are missing Wands—There could be a lack of passion, chemistry, drive, or direction.

- If you are missing Swords—Stagnation, or a lack of boundaries or structure may be problematic. A lack of challenge may lead to boredom. Miscommunication may be present.

- If the reading contains no Major Arcana cards—The situation may feel bigger than it actually is and will have little to no lasting impact.

- If the reading contains no Court cards—There may be a lack of control or leadership in the situation. Additional guidance may be necessary.

- If the reading contains no Minor Arcana cards—This is rare considering how the majority of the deck is the Minor Arcana. But if you only receive Major Arcana cards and no Minor Arcana or Court cards, the situation may be bigger than yourself, impacting several people.

Scott performed a reading for himself when he was trying to lose weight. Getting to his weight goal was tougher and taking longer than he'd anticipated. He wanted to know if something was missing from his health and fitness plan.

Scott used the Present Triangle spread found on page 188.

Scott generally understands the Hierophant to mean "plans and endeavors." He agreed that he had been on a very structured diet and exercise course for a while, as indicated by the Hierophant in the past position. The present situation, the Wheel of Fortune, told him that he was on the right track, although the pace was slow.

"I see the Wheel of Fortune as a slow mover," he said. "It does feel like progress is happening, although it's not on the schedule I want."

For the future, he saw the 2 of Cups to mean possibly getting help or advice from someone else.

Scott sees the Wands as cards of movement, and so in his reading he took them to mean his exercise plan.

The Past

The Present

The Future

Effects of Past on Present

Effects of Present on Future

Root or Truth of Situation

Present Triangle Spread

An injury he suffered in college limited the amount of strenuous exercise he could do over a long period of time. The Knight of Wands reversed, indicating slow movement, made sense in the position of showing effects of the past on the present.

Scott has struggled to understand the Queens in his self-readings in the past, but in this situation he saw the Queen of Wands in reverse as self-criticism. "I may be holding myself back because things aren't happening as fast as I want them to," he said.

Finally, the root cause of the situation was the 4 of Cups. "The answer is there, but I just don't see it yet," he said. Scott hoped that the 2 of Cups in the future was a sign that the answer would reveal itself.

Scott noticed that his reading did not include any Pentacles or Swords. The will and the desire for him to reach his goal were present, as indicated through the inclusion of the Wands and Cups. The presence of two Major Arcana cards signified for him that he was placing rightful attention on his weight-loss goal, without placing too much attention on it. "If I had all Majors, I would think that I was letting the focus on losing weight take up too much space in my life," he said.

But missing Pentacles and Swords left an important message in Scott's reading. "If Pentacles are about the physical world, then they include the body. If my reading on weight loss has no Pentacles, there is something in my routine that isn't right for my body." Scott wondered if the lack of Pentacles was linked to the lack of Swords. "If Swords indicate something happening quickly, no Swords could be present if what I'm doing isn't right for my body. How could anything happen quickly if it's not happening correctly?"

This reading told Scott that the problem wasn't with his willpower, but more with the plan he'd selected for himself. The cards indicated a need to find another solution, and this encouraged him to find a personal trainer and speak to a nutritionist. With the information provided by Tarot, he could speak to these professionals about what other sorts of plans might better suit his body type.

Not Every "Scary" Card Is Bad

No matter how long we've read Tarot, there will always be a few cards we simply don't like to receive in our readings. I am guilty of pulling the Tower or the 10 of Swords as a "card of the day" and saying, "Nope, not today," before sticking it back in the deck and pulling another one. I don't recommend this. First of all, it's a waste of time. Like it or not, the card(s) pulled will manifest anyway. Second, reshuffling and re-dealing tells Tarot we don't trust its voice. Doing this over time will disrupt the language we have built with it. It's better to sigh, grit our teeth, and (pardon the pun) accept the cards we've been dealt.

What I have learned through my teeth-gritting is to consciously dig deeper for the potential blessing in what I personally deem a "scary" card. Each Tarot card has its own gifts, even if that gift is like the strength you get after an intense workout: it sure didn't feel like a gift when you thought you would vomit all over the gym, but the endorphins and increased health in the aftermath were very much a gift you gave yourself.

Tough Major Arcana Cards

The following cards are often seen as tough cards by many readers. You may happen to love some of these cards. I know plenty of excellent readers in deep love affairs with the Devil and some with absolutely no qualms about the Tower. There may be cards you personally despise that I haven't listed below. Suggestions for working with other cards not listed here can be found toward the end of the chapter.

9. The Hermit

THE HERMIT.

This card often scares people, particularly if it surfaces during a love reading. Because of the Hermit's natural association with solitude, it makes sense that it might trigger concerns about a life alone. But the Hermit can mean venturing away from like-minded others, seeking deeper wisdom, and possibly lighting a path for others. The Hermit represents a level of comfort with one's self and individual path. It does not mean you are going to be lonely, alone, and destitute. Even in love readings, it doesn't automatically portend a breakup or a life living solely with cats and not partners, but it can mean an increased focus on yourself as an individual. This may mean it's good to take time for yourself before diving deeper into the dating scene or committing more fully to your partner. In love, we're often encouraged to surrender our identities to the relationship. The Hermit reminds us to hold on to ourselves even as our paths merge with others.

12. The Hanged Man

THE HANGED MAN.

While the Hanged Man indicates being caught, stalled, or otherwise prevented from moving forward on something, it can also be a time of rest. While writing this book, I took three vacation days from my job to work on it. The previous month had been extremely busy, fraught with travel and long days. I was looking forward to getting caught up on my writing; but when I pulled a card to see how the work would go and I got the Hanged Man, I groaned. Something would not line up with my plan. I ended up coming down with a high fever and a chest cold and spent my vacation days sleeping instead of writing. I was upset, very much like how I would imagine the character in the Hanged Man to be. But upon meditating on the character's face, I noticed how serene he appeared. I grudgingly accepted that I needed to stop and rest before I could move forward. While it wasn't easy and I had a hard time getting out of the "I'm wasting so much time being sick!" mind trap, the period of enforced rest helped me move past a few other writing blocks and I ultimately felt better about the course the book took.

The Hanged Man can also barricade against a symbolic cliff's edge. It may be a sign to stop and reflect. It does not mean certain doom and gloom. The Hanged Man can encourage us to delegate responsibility. A few years ago, a friend of mine was in a custody battle over her grandson. The situation was stressing her to the point of illness. She too pulled the Hanged Man in a reading, but instead of focusing on its potential to mean stalls and delays, she accepted the Hanged Man as a sign that she had done all she could in the matter. Nothing more was expected from her. She allowed herself to let go of the situation and felt the peace that can come with this aspect of the Hanged Man. The Hanged Man can encourage us to drop obligations or "the shoulds" that weigh us down. How liberating to be able to say, "I've done all I can," or "I have no power here, so I don't have any choices to make." The irony of the Hanged Man is that there is a true freedom in it. Some stalling, yes. But there is also release.

13. Death

This is probably the most misunderstood card in Tarot. When I read for clients, this is usually the card that scares them the most. Death can and often does mean endings, and sometimes it also signals loss. But it can also mean welcome transitions. A few years ago, one friend of mine did a self-reading and got the Death card. While that naturally might frighten most people, she remained open to a potentially positive outcome. Shortly thereafter, she discovered she was pregnant with her first child. She opted to leave her job and stay home with her baby, which was what she wanted to do. The Death card meant a kind of "death": a transition from full-time employment to caring for a baby full-time. It's also not uncommon for someone to receive Death before a marriage proposal or moving in with a partner. A single person may receive the Death card before entering a new romance. It can signal the end of single life.

The Death card in readings about relationships, career, creative enterprise, or other endeavors does not always mean loss, either. A happy relationship may receive the Death card not as an omen of ill will, but as one of leaving one chapter and entering another. It can also mean dramatic changes within a relationship for the better, such as a move, or a joint decision to forgo bad habits and embrace health. It could be a new way of communication that will ultimately make the partnership stronger. In a career or creative sense, the Death card could portend a promotion, even an opportunity that might mean other endeavors need to wait until the new one takes root.

When we receive the Death card and we focus solely on the loss, we miss its gifts. By being open to its rebirth aspects and the doors that open rather than the doors that have closed, we can find greater potential within our readings.

15. The Devil

It's common to see the Devil as deceit and treachery, and in many cases this is probably the correct interpretation. As we've discussed, the Devil can represent fears, toxic relationships, enemies, repressed issues, and more. However, in the right time and place in your reading, the Devil can be your best friend. If we can imagine for a time that the Devil is not bent on destruction or injury and it does appear in a reading, how might this be a friend to you?

Maybe the Devil is someone who harbors information you need in a situation. Perhaps you are applying for a job and you know someone already working there who can provide information about what the potential employer is looking for. With this information, you can do a little better on the interview. Some may say that's an unfair advantage. Others might argue that we need to use every resource we can to take care of ourselves and those dependent on us. Either way, this is an example of the Devil's tricky but helpful nature. In addition, because the Devil rules the realm of fears, it can take us to scary places within ourselves, encouraging us to challenge them. Many find the Devil concerning in love readings, but it doesn't necessarily mean trouble in the heart. It might be a call from the Devil's advocate, encouraging an objective look at your actions and thinking more about your partner's side of things. On a more sensual note, the Devil can allow us to indulge intimately in a safe, consensual manner.

Storm is a gender-fluid Tarot reader who describes their gender as unlimited and inclusive, expressing itself differently every day. Storm mentioned that for them, the Devil card represents how they confine themselves to traditional gender roles: "For me, the Devil is what is within myself that keeps me in bondage, who responds to societal conditioning with fear and subservience of oppressive or harmful systems. The Devil represents the bondage I put or keep myself in, or how I hold myself down or under as well as the temptation to remain ignorant willfully—even about myself. Unlearning my fear of the Divine, embracing the power of freedom from traditional roles and stereotypes, and unleashing the self-inflicted conformity to the unhelpful gender binary or what I was assigned are all part of what I understand of the Devil card. It's a big part of my struggle on a wider scale. I limit myself constantly in my career and spiritual life, so for me the Devil is an invaluable teacher, reminding me that the world is full of enemies. I needn't be one to myself."

16. The Tower

Just before I published my first book, I had a blog post go viral for the first time. The night before it happened, I dreamed I was standing in my place of work at the time (which was in a tall building) and a tornado ripped through New York City, taking most of the taller buildings out with it, including most of the one I was standing in. In the last part of the dream, I stood in a doorway, one of few parts of the building that still stood, and gazed out on the rubble of the fallen towers all around me and wondered what would happen next. That dream was a subconscious burp that perfectly embodies the Tower card—a great force of nature wiping out man-made structures. For me, the Tower partially represented my place of work (which I ultimately ended up leaving a few months later for something much better suited for me). It also represented the collapse of anonymity. Prior to that dream I enjoyed the freedom of obscurity. But suddenly, my name and words were all over the place and the Tower of obscurity that I had both resented (in wanting success) and clung to (out of fear of people knowing too much about me) was no longer there. Like my dream where I stood in the ruined doorway, I was suddenly exposed to a new world of being known and unsure of what that would ultimately mean for me.

The Tower can best be approached with the mentality of "Bring it on." Unearthing can be scary. It may even hurt. But like the Death card, the possibilities that the Tower presents have the potential to be far more beautiful than if the Tower had not ever come through one's life. Sometimes we have to allow the rubble to fall around us. Sometimes we need to face the destruction. In my dream of tornadoes and falling buildings, there was a bright horizon in the distance. Transitions don't always feel good. In fact, they can often be painful and scary. The bright side of the Tower is the horizon on the other side of it.

What is holding us back? Usually it's something we don't even realize is blocking us. Sometimes we think the collapse is the problem, but the Tower tells us that sometimes the Tower itself was the problem, not the collapse. Maybe we rebuild, or maybe we just walk away. Either way, there's a bright horizon on the other side of the rubble. When we allow this to be the focus of the Tower rather than the demolition dust, we find release and joy.

Challenging Minor Arcana Cards

The images on Minor Arcana cards tip them off as being difficult or not. If you are using a deck other than the RWS, it may likely provide a different system of blessing or challenge.

The 2 of Swords

The 2 of Swords often means we're blinded from the truth—or, more accurately, we're unwilling to accept the truth. This card can be a warning that we're being prevented from knowing certain truths that would help us. But sometimes keeping ourselves blind is better.

Maybe it's better to keep your distance in some situations. What if the character in the 2 of Swords is pulling back from family drama? Maybe a conniving coworker is trying to wrangle you into workplace politics. Maybe the camping trip your friends invited you on will be flooded by heavy rains and it's better to stay home. The 2 of Swords is a useful time for restraint. While for many it may suggest a need to remove the proverbial blindfold and open the self, there will be times when staying out of something might be a better option.

The 3 of Swords

Okay, I'm not going to lie. I really don't like the 3 of Swords. I find it stressful. In the RWS deck, the image of three swords tearing through a heart reminds me of heartbreak and anguish. But a couple of years ago, my Coven did a series of meditations from *Casting Sacred Space* by Ivo Dominguez Jr. The chapter "Four Simple Rituals for Personal Growth" includes personal rituals utilizing the different Threes in the Tarot: the 3 of Wands, the 3 of Cups, the 3 of Swords, and the 3 of Pentacles. As a method of getting to know the challenges and benefits of these four cards, I recommend these exercises. When doing the 3 of Swords exercise, I saw the beauty of this card for the first time. It reminded me of a Purple Heart medal. Perhaps the card is a badge of honor in my readings? Maybe our trials are painful, but we can carry them with pride. Sometimes, when I receive the card, it suggests that the problems I feel I am facing may actually only be that—fallacies of an overworked mind. For me, it is also a reminder of courage but also a sign that the things I may be most worried about perhaps aren't as terrible as I feared.

The 5 of Cups

The cloaked, hovering figure in the 5 of Cups may spell gloom and sadness in some readings. In many of my readings, this card has indeed meant some sort of mourning was present or soon to occur. Yet, sometimes I wonder if that character is truly sad. Are they secretly giggling? Are they sighing in relief? Do the spilled cups behind them contain lethal poisons, and are they offering prayers of thanks for their life? Are they checking a text message from a crush?

Relearning the Tough Cards

Pull a card from the deck that you don't like. List all of the negative things you associate with it. For example, I am not crazy about the 10 of Swords. For it, I would list: defeat, pain, loss, disloyalty.

Next, list an opportunity or benefit that could come from each negative thing. For example, I would list

- ◆ When I am defeated . . . I learn a better way to win next time.

- ◆ When I am in pain . . . I find ways to be strong.

- ◆ When I experience loss . . . I find renewed joy in what I still have.

- ◆ When I experience disloyalty . . . I find clarity in where my true loyalty resides.

For me, receiving the 10 of Swords might mean the negative qualities I listed, but it also may mean strategies, strength, appreciation, and an understanding of whom I can really trust.

Also take note of any thing of beauty in the card. No matter how frightening the image in your particular card might be, look for some sense of bounty. In the 10 of Swords, past the blades in the character's back, I see a sunrise on the other side of some very threatening-looking clouds. I notice how the character is focusing on that as opposed to the scary clouds above. When I see those things, it makes me think of acupuncture. The swords remind me of needles poking into someone in order to heal them—perhaps a grisly sight if you're not familiar with the practice, but one ultimately designed for health.

This exercise is not meant to erase your gut response to these cards. Perhaps the Devil will always mean an enemy and the Tower always disaster. If this is part of your Tarot language, a positive spin will not diminish that. But seeking the potential positive outcome can provide helpful tools for navigating the cards when they come up. When I get the 10 of Swords, my first response will likely be defeat before it will mean strategy to win, but I can be aware of this when the 10 of Swords moment manifests. I can embrace it for the strategically based lessons it has for me rather than only focus on the proverbial swords I feel in my back!

Not Every "Good" Card Is Completely Good

I've seen decks whose artists have turned every difficult card into a gentle card. The Devil is a quasi-joker and the Tower stands tall, firm, and unthreatening. I once heard of a deck in which the traditionally tough cards were omitted altogether. I avoid such decks, as I believe omitting or diminishing the tough cards robs Tarot of its imperative role of showing different facets of human experience. Not every experience will coddle and nurture. Many will be difficult. Even if a difficult experience has a blessed lesson attached, it doesn't always feel good in the moment.

Watch Out for These Potential Warnings

One Tarot truth frequently forgotten is that not every positive card has only positive connotations. Even in the most optimistic card in the deck, there exists the potential for a warning.

The 3 of Cups

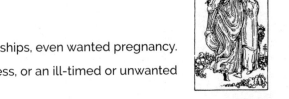

The 3 of Cups often means jubilation, friendships, even wanted pregnancy. It can also mean overindulgence, cliquishness, or an ill-timed or unwanted pregnancy.

The 4 of Wands

The 4 of Wands indicates celebration, coming together, possible marriage. Yet one of my students looked at the RWS version and wondered if the wedding guests were rioting and the married couple running away. Perhaps the union is not a celebrated one.

The 10 of Pentacles

The 10 of Pentacles means wealth and abundance. But does that wealth come with increased taxes or responsibilities? Will the wealth stay around, or will it disappear in the next card?

The Queen of Cups

The Queen of Cups often indicates a loyal or doting partner but may also indicate overbearingness. Sometimes, when I see the Queen of Cups in the RWS deck focusing so diligently on the cup in her hands as she sits at the water's edge, I think of an old Irish myth in which a woman was so very much in love with her husband that she couldn't bear to even be on the other side of the room from him. He felt so smothered that he went to sea and she paced on the water's edge, wailing for him every day. The Queen of Cups has many wonderful interpretations, but being potentially clingy and overwhelming may very well be part of it, also.

The King of Swords

The King of Swords is often a protector or defender of something. This sense of protection can easily merge into being controlling. The desire to defend could translate into abuse, either of others or the person/thing the King of Swords means to defend. It can be a card of knowing whether your desired intentions match their ultimate execution.

The High Priestess

Usually a card of intuition, Spirit, and Magick, as Neo noticed in his reading in chapter 5, the High Priestess can also be a manipulative and two-faced presence. She is meant to sit in a temple of Higher Knowledge, but in the RWS deck we may notice that behind her is a thin veil followed by water, and we wonder how stable this temple truly is. Her robe seems to turn into a rushing river at the bottom. Is the High Priestess bound to fade away?

Strength

The Strength card means just what it says—Strength. That should be good, right? But do we ever stop to notice that in many decks the woman is *sticking her hand into a lion's mouth*? Does she lose that hand in the next frame? Is the poor animal so tame and/or drugged that it makes it safe for a human to do that? The question here is strength over what, and at what cost? If that which does not kill us makes us stronger, what in the world is it that we're experiencing?

The Flip Side of Your Favorite Cards

As in the previous exercise, take a card for which you find a traditionally positive outcome and look at it carefully. Again, list the interpretations you have about this card that make it so positive. For this exercise, I've chosen the World. The interpretations I have include the following: strong finish, positive outcome, joyful conclusion.

As before, list questions you may have for the card about the positive outcomes. List also any potential downfalls such an outcome might have. Here's an example:

♦ If the World means strong finish . . . what cost of that finish?

♦ If it's a positive outcome . . . who will receive that positive outcome? Who won't?

♦ If it's a joyful conclusion . . . will the next chapter be so happy?

With these interpretations, I can still revel in the positive interpretations of the card, but it also allows me to look at things from another and potentially instructive angle. I don't just end the reading on a high note. It leaves me with more information to dig deeper and think broader, such as "This may be good for me, but will it be good for those I care about? Is this joyful conclusion going to lead me into an even tougher situation?"

Remember to look at the card closely. Does it provide any warnings with its joyful message? In the RWS World card, I notice the character is standing on air. Is she likely to fall? I also notice the animals around her. Will they turn around and eat her? She's naked . . . is she cold? Does she even appreciate the position she is in?

Just as the previous exercise is not meant to water down the warning messages of the difficult cards, this exercise is not meant to be pessimistic about the blessing cards. Both of these exercises are designed to show that no single card is all "bad" or completely benevolent. Every situation in life holds both blessings and challenges, but one side of the situation is usually more immediately prevalent. The same is true for Tarot. Whether you receive a comforting or alarming card, know that a flip side is present. Embracing both will enhance your readings.

EIGHT

WHEN NOT TO READ TAROT FOR YOURSELF

Reading for yourself is not always the best option. Sometimes it's better to have others read for you. There will be times when it's best not to consult Tarot at all. Tarot can be addictive. A portal to otherworldly information is irresistible. I know this has been a particularly vulnerable area for me, both when I was new at reading Tarot, and sometimes even now. When I'm unusually worried about something, I want to run right for my cards. I've learned this is the wrong time for me to pick up a deck. Knowing when it makes sense to read your own cards and when it's best to seek another reader or avoid Tarot for a time is a valuable part of self-reading.

Reading About Other People

Some readers believe it's immoral to read about what's going on with someone else. I don't agree. Concerns about family members' health, partners' well-being, children's safety, etc. are very much part of human existence. There is little about us that isn't connected to what's going on in the lives of others. Other questions crucial to personal well-being may include wanting to know about your boss's thoughts about layoffs in the coming year. Other readings may simply provide peace of mind, such as seeing how a son or daughter is doing in college. Still others are simply natural to human curiosity, such as what an ex-lover might be up to. When reading about others, particularly if others' choices have deep implications for our own selves (as in the example of the employer), it can be hard to see outside of our heads. Our fears and desires may cloud our interpretations. In a case like curiosity about an ex-lover, it can be all too easy to fixate on what might be happening with them. We may even find ourselves shuffling and reshuffling the deck to find out more and more information. We can easily confuse ourselves.

Joi, a proficient Tarot reader, asked me to read for them as their self-readings weren't giving them a clear answer. They eagerly wanted to know what their ex thought of them. I pulled a single card to answer the question: the 10 of Pentacles. Joi said, laughing, "Do they think I'm expensive?" My interpretation was not that Joi was expensive, but that the relationship had cost Joi's ex something great—be it emotions, time, or possibly money. Because Joi was quite concerned with whether their ex had loved them or not, they weren't able to see that the former beloved's feelings were more complicated. The breakup was too fresh for Joi to read their own Tarot at that time. Their feelings had clouded their ability to see other options besides "My ex loved me/my ex loved me not" within the cards.

While it's natural to be curious about the actions of others, it can be counterproductive to read about others' feelings during a self-reading. Feelings change, even over the course of a day. You might use Tarot to peek in on a good friend's feelings about you and the cards will indicate nonchalance. However, this doesn't mean your friend is *always* nonchalant about you. You might be doing your reading at a moment in which they were thinking about picking up their dry cleaning. Their thoughts were simply on something other than yourself. This might leave you with a wrong impression. In addition, using Tarot to find out another person's thoughts and feelings is a quick route to a feedback loop of obsession. Years ago, I had a client who wanted to know what her estranged husband thought of her. After pulling a card to answer that question, the client wanted to know what her husband thought of a female coworker. Then she wanted to know if he thought of her when in the presence of that coworker . . . and then she wanted to know if he thought of the coworker when he visited my client, etc. The questions went on and on until she finally took my deck out of my hand and began pulling cards, over and over, in search of an answer to her ex-husband's enigmatic thoughts and feelings. Each card only made her more confused and frustrated.

This experience taught me to pose questions that will lead to enriching answers. I'm not immune to tapping Tarot when I want to know what someone is thinking. Be it for peace of mind or our own self-preservation, there are times we simply want to know what's going with other people. But before we overanalyze nebulous answers, let's start with formulating questions that provide more solid responses.

Instead of . . .	Try . . .
What does my ex think of me?	What steps can I take to establish a better friendship with my ex and/or move on from thinking about this person?
Am I going to get fired from my job?	In what ways could I be better at my job? What sorts of opportunities are out there if I decided to look for other work?
What is my child up to at school?	How can I be a better support system for my child?

When You're Deeply Worried About Something

Like most Tarot readers I know, there comes a time when you really, really need to know something, and at any given point you may become obsessed with knowing the outcome. I guess that is true for most humans. But Tarot readers have the special ability to drive themselves absolutely mad in the search for the best outcome. As I write this, I'm remembering how I used to obsess about a failing romance, flipping cards over and over again to find out if the relationship would work out. Despite my years of experience with Tarot, I could not see through my worries about the relationship to understand what the cards said. I routinely ended up in a flood of angry, confused, and tired tears.

When we are worried, we are blinded by our fears that things will not turn out in the way that we want. Any cards we pull that do not relate to our desired outcome will look like bad omens and will make us feel worse.

Years ago, when I was producing *Tarot of the Boroughs*, I had booked a photo shoot with a very famous person. I was terrified that something would come up and that this person would be unable to make it. The night before the shoot, I did a self-reading and asked how things would go. This was a mistake. I pulled the 3 of Swords and was even more worried than before my reading. Would the model abandon the shoot? Would the model not like the shoot? Would something else go wrong? My fears drained my ability to sleep, and I was zombified all day during the shoot. The model arrived on time, the lighting was great, all was okay, but I bumbled and fumbled and was embarrassed. My self-reading had reflected my own stress about the situation and added to it. I was far worse off than had I simply gone through with the shoot without having done the self-reading.

During the process of writing this book, I was also planning my wedding. As is common in the wedding-planning process, there were a few times when things did not go so well. Stress, arguments, and things falling through made me wonder how things would go on the big day. Sometimes, I was tempted to consult Tarot about whether the wedding would proceed without a disastrous meltdown, but I did not self-read because I was already too worried. This was an instance in which I sought a reading from someone else because I knew my own fears and worries would cloud my ability to read for myself clearly.

If you simply can't resist and you decide to do a reading on the thing that's worrying you, take care in how you phrase your questions. Simply asking, "How will X fare?" or "Will I/won't I?" is likely to leave you unhappy and confused by your reading. Consider reshaping your questions as below:

Instead of . . .	Try . . .
Will I get the job I applied for?	Will I find gainful employment that satisfies me, and in short time?
Will I ever find love?	How can I bring romantic love into my life?
Will I ever be happy?	What steps can I take to make myself happy?

When You Are Feeling Depressed

Tarot is helpful, but it doesn't coddle. If you are feeling depressed and are looking to Tarot to alleviate that feeling, you might end up with a cushy 10 of Cups to tell you that everything is going to be okay. But you might also get a 10 of Swords that says, "Nope. You're pretty screwed right now." Before doing a self-reading, ask yourself if you're in a place where you could handle receiving the latter. If you think getting tougher cards would only depress you further instead of challenge you to make changes, it's not the right time to do a self-reading. Seeking out a reader you trust might be helpful. If you are dealing with serious depression, grief, or anxiety, it might be best to avoid Tarot all together until these conditions are managed. Even the most positive reading might not be well received or understood when one is seriously depressed.

If you feel that a reading would be helpful but you are not in the state to do it, seek out another reader. Be selective about who reads for you when you are feeling down. If you've not seen a particular reader before, consider contacting them ahead of time and let them know you are in a vulnerable state. When you're feeling better, you might prefer a reader who is more direct. A qualified reader will take your needs into consideration. If they're not able to help you, they may be able to suggest someone who can.

But for those of you who simply aren't going to listen and will go ahead and read for yourselves in the midst of your deepest blues . . . here are some thoughts: Rather than seeking a specific answer from Tarot (such as will my life ever not suck so much?), use Tarot as a tool to help get yourself back on track to emotional well-being. When I have waded through my own pools of depression, I stop seeking specific answers through Tarot. Instead, I use Tarot this way:

If I Pull a Major Arcana Card

I will pose as that card until I just might feel like it's part of me. For this exercise, I ignore the cards that generally trouble me, such as the Devil or the Tower. If the card I pull is the Magician, I will stand with one hand above my head, envisioning that I am holding the scroll with all the information I could ever need in this world to make myself feel better, and with my hand reaching downward I envision all the pain and suffering I am going through to be channeled out of the pointed finger into the earth below. The last time I did this, I found myself wont to move into John Travolta dance moves from *Saturday Night Fever*. If it sounds silly, it's because it is—and that's the point. Tarot isn't stoic. It likes to make us laugh. The tiny movements can get us out of our heads and help bust up a mental funk. We can embody the power of the Magician, the warmth of the Sun, and the carry-onward presence of the Wheel of Fortune.

If I Pull a Minor Arcana Card

I will use it as a tool to count my blessings. For example, should I pull the 8 of Wands, I would list eight things that excite me—even if those things are as banal as eating peanut butter or petting my cat. The 4 of Cups might be four ways I know I am loved. The 9 of Swords could be nine things over which I know I have no control. The 2 of Pentacles suggests two things I can do to make myself feel a little better such as taking a walk or watching a hilarious movie.

If I Pull a Court Card

I will reflect on a time in which I embodied what I know to be the greatest possible persona of that card. If I were to pull the Knight of Wands, I might reflect on my time leading a large Pagan group at the People's Climate March. I circulated information, kept us moving, even led impromptu rituals in Times Square—all while battling a chest cold. This was the best example of me being a Knight of Wands, channeling the power I had to help give people direction in support of an important cause. It gives me strength to know that if such an experience was in me at one point, it could be found again.

When You Only Want a Very Specific Answer

I'm mentioning this again because I don't think it can be stressed enough when it comes to Tarot: *Seek answers from Tarot when you are receptive to whatever answers those might be—not only when you are seeking one specific answer.* Tarot knows things that we don't, but sometimes we're not ready to hear them. Say you were in the tough situation of needing to re-home a pet. You think you've found the right home for this pet, but things haven't been finalized. Because you care about your pet, you desperately want it to work. But if you seek Tarot hoping it will say, "9 of Cups! Your pet will be happy in this home forever!" and instead get "8 of Cups: Keep searching . . ." you might panic. You may want so badly for the home you've found to be the right place for sweet little Max or Lucy, but Tarot isn't convinced.

What if Tarot is picking up on the possibility that the first home wasn't really the right one? What if you take the advice of the 8 of Cups and find an even better home for your fur baby? You may not want to hear it, but Tarot is not built for telling anyone what they want to hear, but rather what is best for them to know.

Sometimes we think we know what we want, but the Universe is cooking up something that will make us even happier. If we're too mired in our desires to hear one specific thing, we may be upset with hearing otherwise and start trying to change the situation instead of simply letting the blessings come to us in whatever forms they may appear. Again, seek Tarot when you are ready to hear the right answers, not only the answers you want to hear.

If you are only seeing negative outcomes in your reading, it might not be the right time to consult the cards. If you can't see a positive outcome, seek a reading from someone else. Ask them to record the reading, and listen to it later. I've read for some people who, no matter how much hope I infuse into my interpretations, walk away feeling "permanently screwed," as one of my friends is known to say. When this happens, I suggest they listen to the recording after giving themselves a little more time and distance from the reading. If they still can't hear anything positive in the reading, then it might be time for them to take a break from consulting Tarot altogether. This can be a sign to seek out help from a mental health provider, as it could be a sign of depression.

When You Find Yourself Asking the Same Question Over and Over Again

Many years ago, I spent a weekend with a friend. She was a nervous wreck about whether or not to take a job and wanted to consult Tarot about it. She shuffled and re-dealt the cards over and over again for hours, asking the same question each time. Finally, she got all swords and thought this final reading spelled disaster. I took it to mean that the cards were tired of answering the same question and suggested she leave Tarot alone for a while.

If you find that you keep tweaking your question in the hopes that you'll receive a different outcome (Will we get pregnant this year? Will we get pregnant within twelve months from today? Will we get pregnant within twelve months of when we hoped to get pregnant?), chances are that you are too attached to the outcome. It's probably a good time to step away from the cards, but if you still want to read, lay your spread and take a photo of it. Don't look too deeply into it, and then put the cards away for a few days. When you're ready to be open to Tarot's message, review the photo to see what the images now say to you.

When You Are Tired

A fatigued Tarot reader is rarely an insightful Tarot reader. Even if you are dying for insight on something, it's better to read Tarot when you're fresh and rested. Tired Tarot readings are usually confusing and can be stressful. In addition, you're likely to be more emotional and focused on a specific outcome rather than being open to the true message. If you just can't stand it, consider doing the above and taking a picture of the reading, focusing on it again when you're better rested.

When You Are Upset

Welling up in tears during a reading can be a sign of great synchronicity, but reaching for your deck when you're already in a flood of tears is not grounds for a good reading. Tarot shouldn't be the place you run to when you're already distraught. When we are distraught, hearing anything other than "It's going to be okay" will hurt more than help, and, as we've discussed, Tarot isn't always going to tell us what we want to hear. Cry it out. Call a friend or partner. Take a bath. Listen to music you love. Return to Tarot when you are calm, balanced, and truly ready to hear its message.

Be Careful with Obsession

As mentioned earlier, if you find yourself asking basically the same question over and over again in different forms, you need to take a break. Remember, the greatest risk in Tarot is not any sort of moral risk, but addiction. If you find yourself consulting Tarot about *every* decision you need to make, you are becoming too dependent. A healthy limit is one reading a day *maximum* with a limited number of questions—one question with perhaps a clarifying or follow-up question should be sufficient. This is a good practice for anyone with an interest in reading Tarot, but if you are a particularly obsessive person (. . . I raise my hand from behind my computer screen . . .), it is important to impose specific limits on yourself. Otherwise, you will confuse, frustrate, and rob yourself of the power of trusting your intuition and the practice of confident decision making. Limits on your self-readings are for your own good!

The Moral of the Story

Tarot needs an open, balanced, and calm mind to efficiently deliver its messages. We do not need to be in perfect emotional health, but we can't reach for the cards in the middle of a good cry, either. Again, it is best to consult Tarot for tools and clues as opposed to specific yes or no answers about your future. While it does seem as though there are tides of fate that are unavoidable for each person, our futures are generally determined by the choices we make on a daily basis, fed by the information we have at the time we make them. Tarot can provide additional information, such as "If you take this job, here's what you can expect to be challenging" or "If you marry this person, here's how your future is likely to be blessed." Tarot is less effective at telling you whether you'll take the job or marry the person. That choice is yours, and Tarot cannot tell whether you'll make the choice or not; but it can tell you what you might expect as a result of that choice.

Not sure whether it's a good time to consult Tarot? Ask Tarot!

Knowing whether you're in a good frame of mind to read Tarot is a bit like knowing when you're hungry or in love: if you're not sure, you probably aren't. However, you can still consult Tarot to find out if you *should* consult Tarot.

Most Tarot decks include characters that are either open to embracing something or they are closed off. If a card has a more open stance, then the cards are open to reading for you at that time. If the card is closed off, imagine that the cards' closed sign is up.

Here are a few examples:

Open for Business!

Not now.

We (or you) need to rest.

Fire away!

Bring it.

Nope.

If you have a deck that does not include characters with obvious open or closed postures, the following table (using the Major Arcana) can help:

Yes, Go Ahead and Read	No, Hold Off for a Time
0 The Fool	9 The Hermit
1 The Magician	12 The Hanged Man
2 The High Priestess	13 Death
3 The Empress	15 The Devil
4 The Emperor	16 The Tower
5 The Hierophant	18 The Moon
6 The Lovers	
7 The Chariot	
8 Strength	
10 The Wheel of Fortune	
11 Justice	
14 Temperance	
17 The Star	
19 The Sun	
20 Judgment	
21 The World	

As always, these are guidelines and suggestions, not rules. Perhaps you really dislike the Hierophant, or you are typically confused by the Star card. Maybe you love the Tower and the Devil. You may find that a card you typically resonate with is a good go-ahead card *for you* even if my little chart says it's not a great go-ahead card.

You can also reference the Yes/No spread on page 175 to see if it's the right time to do a reading.

NINE

PRACTICE SPREADS

These Tarot spreads, some classic and some original, may be helpful in your self-readings. Unless otherwise specified, the cards in these spreads should be drawn at random

Past/Present/Future: A Three-Card Reading

Card 1	Card 2	Card 3
The Past	The Present	The Future

This is a simple reading to focus on a single question—what happened in the past, what's happening in the present, and what's likely to happen in the future.

Present Triangle

This is an extended version of the simple past/present/future reading. All cards are random pulls.

```
┌──────────┐    ┌──────────┐    ┌──────────┐
│          │    │          │    │          │
│  Card 1  │    │  Card 2  │    │  Card 3  │
│   Past   │    │ Present  │    │  Future  │
│          │    │          │    │          │
└──────────┘    └──────────┘    └──────────┘

      ┌──────────┐    ┌──────────┐
      │          │    │          │
      │  Card 4  │    │  Card 5  │
      │Effects of│    │Effects of│
      │ Past on  │    │ Present  │
      │ Present  │    │ on Future│
      │          │    │          │
      └──────────┘    └──────────┘

           ┌──────────┐
           │          │
           │  Card 6  │
           │Root or   │
           │Truth of  │
           │question  │
           │or        │
           │situation │
           │          │
           └──────────┘
```

Hidden Meaning Reading:
When Something Seems Odd or Off

If you've got the feeling that something isn't right in any given situation, pick three cards to signify where that weird feeling might be coming from.

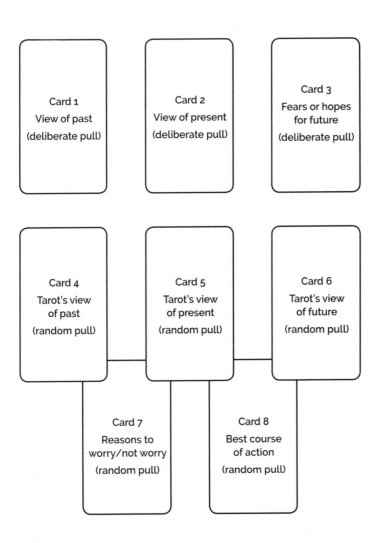

Card 1
View of past
(deliberate pull)

Card 2
View of present
(deliberate pull)

Card 3
Fears or hopes
for future
(deliberate pull)

Card 4
Tarot's view
of past
(random pull)

Card 5
Tarot's view
of present
(random pull)

Card 6
Tarot's view
of future
(random pull)

Card 7
Reasons to
worry/not worry
(random pull)

Card 8
Best course
of action
(random pull)

The Celtic Cross Spread

This is a more common Tarot spread. It is a good reading to forecast current events and those three to six months out.

Card 2
Thoughts and concerns

Card 10
Final outcome
(or events 6-10 months out)

Card 9
Your hopes and fears

Card 4
Recent events
(3-6 months prior)

Card 1
Current situation

Card 5
Future events
(3-6 months ahead)

Card 6
What's crossing you
(what is holding you back or influencing you greatly—positively or negatively)

Card 8
Outside influences

Card 3
Origins of situation

Card 7
Other current circumstances

Daily Oracle Spread

A more involved look at the daily card spread.

Pull five cards at random:

Card 1
Theme of day

Card 2
Opportunities
of the day

Card 3
Restrictions
of the day

Card 4
Things
to avoid

Card 4
Things
to embrace

Goal Seeking Reading

If you are working toward a specific goal in mind, this spread is designed to help plot the course to achieve it.

Deliberately select a card that best depicts your desired outcome.

Desired
Outcome
(deliberate pull)

Shuffle that card back into the mix. Flip through the deck until you find the card you chose. Take note of the two cards surrounding your desired outcome card. Remove all three from deck:

Card behind

Past events/
influences

Desired
Outcome
(deliberate pull)

Card ahead

Future events/
influences

Pull three more cards from the deck at random:

Card 1

What holds
you back

Card 2

What aids you

Card 3

Where your
focus belongs

Conflict Resolution

A spread to solve a conflict.

```
┌──────────────┐
│              │
│              │
│   Current    │
│  situation   │
│(deliberate pull)│
│              │
│              │
└──────────────┘
```

Will it resolve soon? Three cards upright—yes. Two up, one down—probably. Two down, one up—probably not. Three down—no.

```
┌──────────┐   ┌──────────┐   ┌──────────┐
│          │   │          │   │          │
│  Card 1  │   │  Card 2  │   │  Card 3  │
│Random pull│  │Random pull│  │Random pull│
│          │   │          │   │          │
└──────────┘   └──────────┘   └──────────┘
```

How will the situation resolve? Randomly pull three more cards for best course of action.

```
┌──────────┐   ┌──────────┐   ┌──────────┐
│          │   │          │   │          │
│  Card 4  │   │  Card 5  │   │  Card 6  │
│Random pull│  │Random pull│  │Random pull│
│          │   │          │   │          │
└──────────┘   └──────────┘   └──────────┘
```

Soothe the Soul

If something is troubling you and you'd like Tarot to help, this self-reading using both deliberate and random pulls can be helpful.

Card 1
Your view of your situation
(deliberate pull)

Card 2
Your worst fears
(deliberate pull)

Card 5
Real worst-case scenario
(random pull)

Card 3
Your great hopes
(deliberate pull)

Card 6
Feasibility of your greatest hopes
(random pull)

Card 4
What you see as an obstacle
(deliberate pull)

Card 7
True obstacle
(random pull)

Card 8
Reality of your situation
(random pull)

Checking In: Four Quarters Spread

This reading is best used with no particular question in mind, but simply to find out what's going on in the different areas of your life.

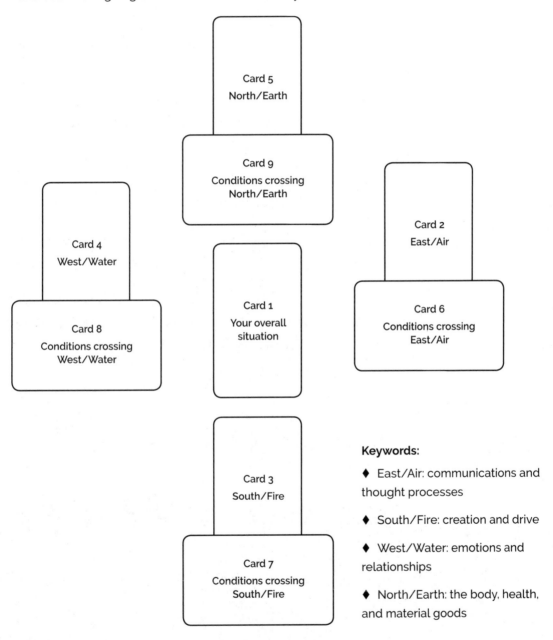

Card 5
North/Earth

Card 9
Conditions crossing
North/Earth

Card 4
West/Water

Card 8
Conditions crossing
West/Water

Card 1
Your overall
situation

Card 2
East/Air

Card 6
Conditions crossing
East/Air

Card 3
South/Fire

Card 7
Conditions crossing
South/Fire

Keywords:

♦ East/Air: communications and thought processes

♦ South/Fire: creation and drive

♦ West/Water: emotions and relationships

♦ North/Earth: the body, health, and material goods

How Long?

If you're looking for an answer regarding time, this spread can help. It does not offer specific dates, but it does offer an idea of events that may surround a desired outcome.

In this spread, the Fool equals the beginning and the World equals the desired outcome. Shuffle the deck.

- ♦ When you have finished shuffling, look through the deck to see where the Fool and the World have landed. Remove them and all cards between them.

- ♦ Remove any cards that came out reversed. If you find the Fool or the World reversed, turn them upright.

- ♦ Imagine that the cards between the Fool and the World mark the events that are to come between the beginning of your search for the outcome and the actual outcome itself.

Example: Jason wants to buy a home. He shuffled the deck and found the following upright cards between the Fool and the World:

In my experience with this reading, each card between the Fool and the World represents a unit of time: days, weeks, months, or years. In the reading, you'll want to look for a reasonable time frame for each card. If Jason were to buy a house in three days, it's possible he's skipping inspections or rushing in on a seemingly good deal without doing sufficient research. It's possible he could buy a house in three weeks, but it's still a stretch. The reasonable expectation is that Jason is going to reach his goal in three months.

The 3 of Wands: Jason will need to seek something—possibly help from a realtor.

The 9 of Wands: Jason may find himself struggling to find something he likes within his price range. It may not be as easy as he'd hoped.

The 5 of Cups: The disappointment may indicate that Jason feels a little discouraged by month three. It's a sign to him to hang in there because the goal is in reach, but the path will not be easy.

Project Success: Will My Venture Be Successful?

This spread can also apply to job searches, relationship repairs, or anything where there is energy invested and success desired.

This is a large spread involving 15 cards, and the layout is shown on page 226.

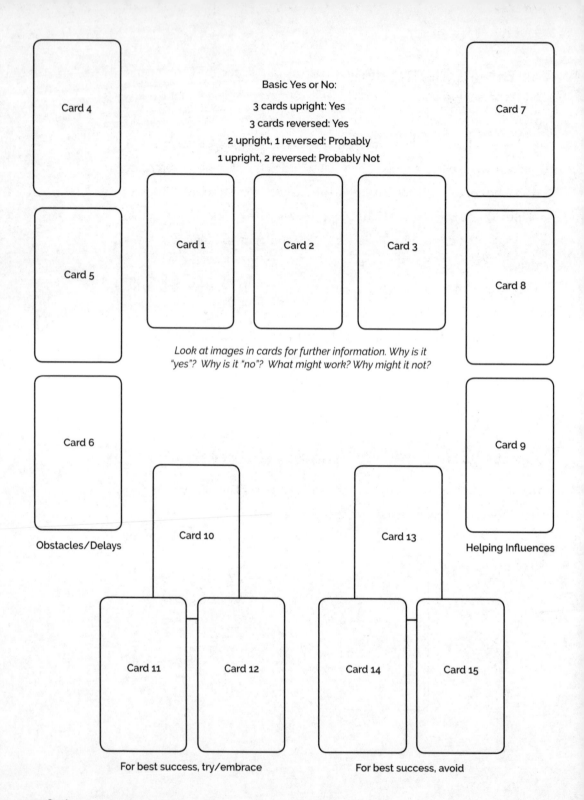

Basic Yes or No:

3 cards upright: Yes

3 cards reversed: Yes

2 upright, 1 reversed: Probably

1 upright, 2 reversed: Probably Not

Card 4

Card 7

Card 1

Card 2

Card 3

Card 5

Card 8

Look at images in cards for further information. Why is it "yes"? Why is it "no"? What might work? Why might it not?

Card 6

Card 9

Obstacles/Delays

Card 10

Card 13

Helping Influences

Card 11

Card 12

Card 14

Card 15

For best success, try/embrace

For best success, avoid

The Three Souls Reading

This spread can help you to find out why something isn't working or to discover influences affecting the situation.

Card 1
Higher Soul

Influences of the Higher Power (aka: God, the Holy Guardian Angel, the Higher Self, the Universe, etc.)

Card 2
Middle Soul

Influences of the Waking Self (the person in the conscious "Now"). How you are helping or hindering yourself.

Card 3
Lower Soul

Influences of the Ancestors, Past Lives or Previous Karma, and societal influences you may be unaware of.

A Couple's Reading

If you are in a relationship, you may eventually ask yourself, "How is my relationship going?" This spread can help. Assign one column for each partner. The horizontal cards suggest shared experiences. Take note of the horizontal cards. A majority pointing in one direction indicates one person giving or taking too much. Having an equal number pointing horizontally means equal footing.

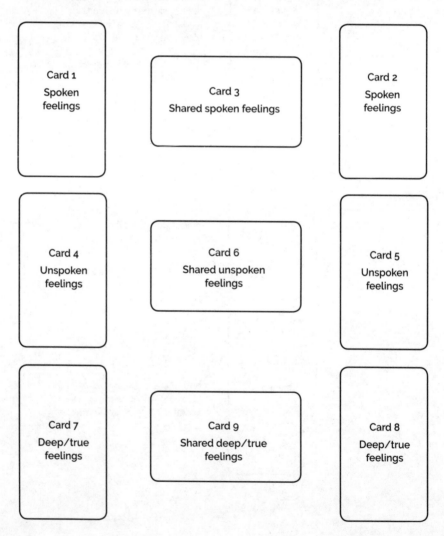

For polyamorous situations, lay a three-card column for each partner and additional shared cards so that one card can reveal how each partner is connecting. Depending on the number of persons, you may need to be creative with how the cards are laid out.

To Work Out a Problem

If this spread highlights a problem in the relationship, pull three more cards:

Card 10

Actions to embrace

Card 12

What would be prudent to discuss

Card 11

Actions to avoid

Forecast for the Coming Week

This spread provides a general theme for each day of the coming week.

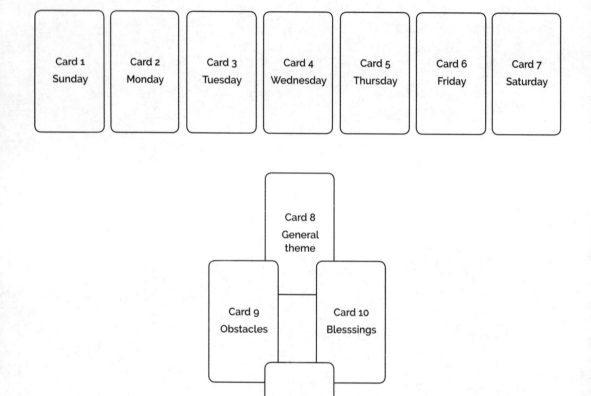

For a Monthly Forecast

The three cards pulled for each week indicate from left to right: Blessing, Challenge, General Theme (bottom). Include the four-card spread from the previous exercise for the general overview of the month.

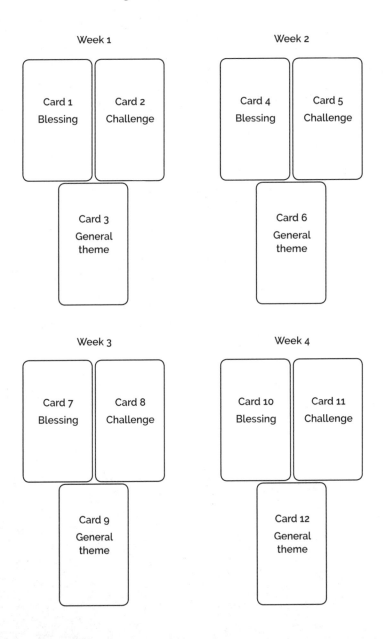

Week 1

Card 1
Blessing

Card 2
Challenge

Card 3
General theme

Week 2

Card 4
Blessing

Card 5
Challenge

Card 6
General theme

Week 3

Card 7
Blessing

Card 8
Challenge

Card 9
General theme

Week 4

Card 10
Blessing

Card 11
Challenge

Card 12
General theme

Seasonal Forecast

For each season, the bottom left card is the blessing, the bottom right is the challenge, and the top of triangle is the unexpected. The crowning card (above the triangle) is the soul's lesson for the season. The center card, the seventeenth card, is the soul's lesson for the year.

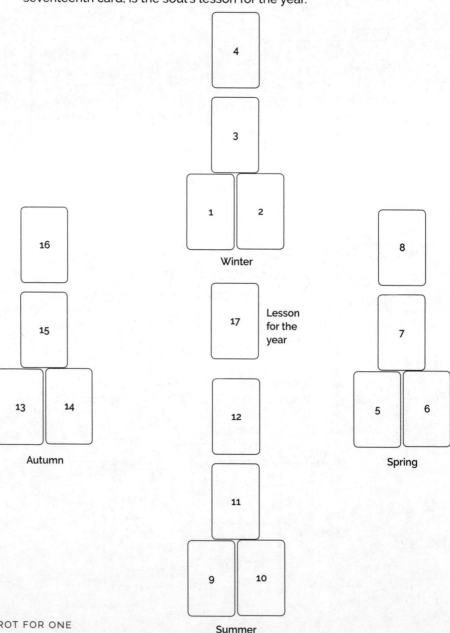

Follow the Wand

This spread uses the Ace of Wands to gain insight into how to develop passions. Shuffle the Ace of Wands (or Staves, Rods, etc.) into the deck. Flip through the deck until you find it, and notice what cards surround it.

Card behind the Ace:

Motivating factors; where to find inspiration

Card on top of the Ace:

Where to direct that energy

Grounding influences for centering

(random pull)

What could help you reach goal

(random pull)

Potential distraction

(random pull)

New Opportunities Spread: Do I Take It or Not?

All cards in this spread are pulled randomly.

Card 5

Sacrifices made or things left behind

Card 4

Your hopes/ fears

Card 6

Blessings not yet seen

Card 2

Past influences: what would be left behind

Card 1

The nature of the opportunity

Card 3

Future influences: what would be gained in the future

Card 7

Soul card: how your soul feels about your opportunity

Card 8

"Freeing card"

Freedom from something left behind

Card 9

Potential obstacles unseen

Read Between the Lines:
Offers, Promotions, Partnerships

You've been offered an opportunity: a job, a move, a collaboration, or even a relationship. This reading will offer more information.

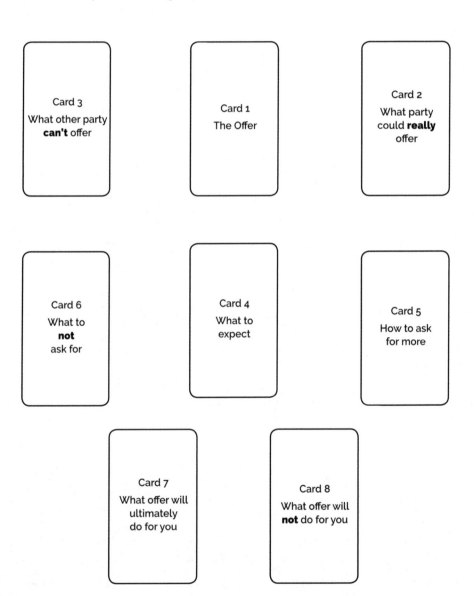

Card 3
What other party **can't** offer

Card 1
The Offer

Card 2
What party could **really** offer

Card 6
What to **not** ask for

Card 4
What to expect

Card 5
How to ask for more

Card 7
What offer will ultimately do for you

Card 8
What offer will **not** do for you

Realizing Passions

You know what you love and want; now how do you make it bloom? For romance or other desires, this spread will show you how to make it happen.

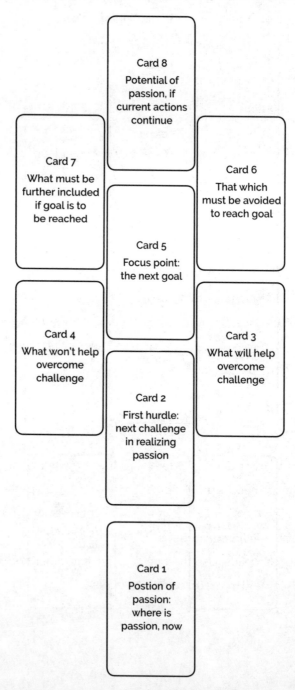

Card 8

Potential of passion, if current actions continue

Card 7

What must be further included if goal is to be reached

Card 6

That which must be avoided to reach goal

Card 5

Focus point: the next goal

Card 4

What won't help overcome challenge

Card 3

What will help overcome challenge

Card 2

First hurdle: next challenge in realizing passion

Card 1

Postion of passion: where is passion, now

AFTERWORD

So . . . that's about it! I hope you enjoyed reading this book as much as I enjoyed writing it. Even more so, I hope you now feel a little more confident about reading your own Tarot. Keep this in mind: Reading one's own Tarot is a craft, and it takes practice, practice, and practice. You're not supposed to be good at it the first time you try it. Try and try again. Make as many mistakes as possible—it's the best way to learn. Make notes and be observant as your readings manifest. Be willing to ignore what this book has said if it conflicts with what you learned to be true in your own readings.

I'll leave you with these last thoughts:

Not every scary reading is meant to spell doom forever. Readings show a very narrow snapshot of what is to come. If the reading looks scary, know it likely won't be as bad as you imagine when it arrives.

Not every positive reading is a sign that we can drop our work and just let the Universe take care of things. We still need to be active participants in our own happiness.

Try different Tarot decks. I referenced the RWS in my examples, but only for reasons of accessibility—not because I think it's a better deck. Trying lots of decks allows new decks to teach you deeper symbolism and messages about readings in general.

Try different spreads. Use the ones I listed, find other books that offer spreads, go crazy and make up some for yourself.

Take notes. You'll be surprised to know how much your reading predicted and how accurate it really was.

Be gentle, patient, and loving with yourself. Celebrate your successes with Tarot, and don't use your mistakes as a barometer of your overall abilities as a reader.

Above all, enjoy Tarot.

Thank you for reading!

Acknowledgments

This book is dedicated to my best friend, Tiffany Spaulding, who gave me my first Tarot deck as a birthday present.

I also want to thank a lady who called herself Walking Woman at Crystal Heart bookstore in Beaverton, Oregon, the first professional reader I ever saw. Wherever she is, she started an unwitting Fool on a powerful journey that day.

Thank you to all who tested these exercises and gave me permission to share gems of their journeys in this book. I offer thanks also to every person who has sought me for a reading or attended one of my classes—you've each taught me far more than you realize.

For their support, information, and inspiration, gratitude goes out to Ruth Ann and Wald Amberstone, Nancy Antenucci, Khi Armand, Stella Dance, Jadzia and Jay DeForest, Shannon Fleischman-Nee, Sasha Graham, Amber Guetebier, Mary Greer, Gemma McGowan, Barbara Moore, Hilary Parry, Robert Place, Rachel Pollack, Theresa Reed, Gina Thies, and Thalassa Therese.

Thank you to the communities of The Reader's Studio, the Bay Area Tarot Symposium, and the Northwest Tarot Symposium. Thank you to my colleagues at Auburn Theological Seminary for their continued support of my work. A special thank you to the members of the Queer Witch Collective, an intersectional safer space for Witches who are queer and/or trans. Thank you to the staff at Weiser Books for this wonderful opportunity, and to Judika Illes for her kind support and encouragement. I give thanks and honor to the memories of Arthur Edward Waite and Pamela Coleman Smith whose work continues to inspire me and other readers.

Thanks and love to my family: Eric and Patti Weber; Meredith, Nate, Westley, and Alexandra Gordon. Finally, the deepest of thanks to my husband, Brian, for his continued support, faith, and love.

Notes

Chapter 1: Welcome to the Self-Read

1 Angeles Arrien, *The Tarot Handbook: Practical Applications of Ancient Visual Symbols* (Sonoma, CA: Arcus Publishing Company, 1987), 16.

2 Isabel Radow Kliegman, *Tarot and the Tree of Life: Finding Everyday Wisdom in the Minor Arcana* (Wheaton, IL: The Theosophical Publishing House), xii.

3 Robert M. Place, *Tarot: History, Symbolism, and Divination* (New York: Penguin Group, 2005), 16–17.

4 Ibid., 9.

5 Ibid., 10.

6 Angeles Arrien, *The Tarot Handbook*, 16.

7 The Cloisters Museum, *The World in Play: Luxury Playing Cards 1430–1540*, The Metropolitan Museum of Art, New York, January 20–April 17, 2016.

8 Ibid.

9 Place, *Tarot*, 9.

10 *Magick* with a *k* is the spiritual practice of change and/or revelation through synchronicity, ritual, or other forms of energy work. *Magic* spelled without the *k* generally refers to illusion-type tricks or parlor magic.

Chapter 2: The Fool's Journey

1 Further information can be found in the "Moon" chapter in *Tarot Wisdom: Spiritual Teachings and Deeper Meanings* by Rachel Pollack (Woodbury, MN: Llewellyn, 2008).

2 Robert V. O'Neill, *Tarot Symbolism* (Lima, OH: Fairway Press, 1986), 32.

3 A. E. Waite, *The Pictorial Key to the Tarot* (Stamford, CT: U.S. Games, 1995), 148–151.

4 Ibid., 151.

5 Oswald Wirth, *The Tarot of the Magicians* (York Beach, ME: Samuel Weiser, 1985), 150.

Chapter 3: Court Cards

1 Gender nonconforming (GNC) persons do not embrace assumptions on how they should look or act based on the gender they were assigned at birth. Some GNC persons may identify with a gender other than their birth gender, as more than one gender, or no gender at all.

2   For excellent resources on traditional meanings, see *General Book of the Tarot* by A. E. Thierens (1930) and *The Tarot Revealed* by Eden Gray (1988).

3   A. E. Waite, *The Pictorial Key to the Tarot* (Stamford, CT: U.S. Games, 1995), 166.

4   My deck is called Tarot of the Boroughs, and at the time of this writing it can be found on my website, *www.thecocowitch.com*.

5   This exercise was inspired by the Court Card Archetypes exercise in Nancy Antenucci's *Psychic Tarot* (Woodbury, MN: Llewellyn, 2011), 35–39.

6   This exercise was inspired by "The Court Within" chapter in Mary Greer and Tom Little's *Understanding the Tarot Court* (Woodbury, MN: Llewellyn, 2004).

Chapter 4: Numbered Cards of the Minor Arcana

1   Variations of descriptions taken from *777 and Other Qabalistic Writings of Aleister Crowley*; *General Book of the Tarot* by A.E. Thierens and Arthur Edward Waite; *Tarot Symbolism* by Robert V. O'Neill; *The Tarot Book* by Jana Riley; *21 Ways to Read a Tarot Card* by Mary K. Greer; and *A Deck of Spells: Hoodoo Playing Card Magic in Rootwork and Conjure* by Professor Charles Porterfield.

2   A. E. Waite, *The Pictorial Key to the Tarot* (Stamford, CT: U.S. Games, 1995), 169.

Chapter 5: Recognizing the Voice of Tarot

1   Scrying is a form of mediumship in which an object (a mirror, a crystal ball, or even stones or a pool of water) is used for focus to retrieve messages from the Spirit world.

2   St. Cyprian is a Catholic Saint, often petitioned by those doing Magick for help in their spellwork. More information can be found at *www.luckymojo.com/saintcyprian.html*.

Chapter 6: Reversed Cards

1   I first heard of this spread in *Tarot Spreads: Layouts & Techniques to Empower Your Readings* by Barbara Moore. She credits Mary K. Greer's *Tarot for Yourself* for this spread.

Chapter 7: Other Tools: What's Missing from Your Tarot Reading?

1   See *www.thetarotlady.com/what-cards-are-saying-when-they-aren't-there/*.

Bibliography

Antenucci, Nancy. *Psychic Tarot.* Woodbury, MN: Llewellyn, 2011.

Coyle, T. Thorne. *Kissing the Limitless.* San Francisco: Red Wheel/Weiser, 2009.

Crowley, Aleister. *777 and Other Qabalistic Writings of Aleister Crowley.* York Beach, ME: Weiser Books, 1986. First edition.

Dominguez Jr., Ivo. *Casting Sacred Space: The Core of All Magickal Work.* San Francisco: Weiser Books, 2012.

Fiebig, Johannes, and Evelin Bürger. *The Ultimate Guide to the Waite Tarot.* Woodbury, MN: Llewellyn, 2013.

Finkel, Michael. "The Last Real Hermit." *GQ.* August 4, 2014.

Fontana, David. *The Essential Guide to the Tarot.* London: Duncan Baird, 2011.

Gray, Eden. *The Tarot Revealed: A Modern Guide to Reading the Tarot Cards.* New York: Bell Publishing Company, 1960.

Greer, Mary K. *21 Ways to Read a Tarot Card.* Woodbury, MN: Llewellyn, 2006.

———. *Tarot for Your Self: A Workbook for Personal Transformation.* Franklin Lakes, NJ: New Page Books, 2002.

Harrow, Judy. *Spiritual Mentoring: A Pagan Guide.* Toronto, Ontario, Canada: ECW Press, 2002.

Holy Bible, Placed by the Gideons, Book of Job.

Moore, Barbara. *Tarot Spreads: Layouts & Techniques to Empower Your Readings.* Woodbury, MN: Llewellyn, 2012.

O'Neill, Robert V. *Tarot Symbolism.* Lima, OH: Fairway Press, 1986.

Place, Robert M. *The Tarot: History, Symbolism, and Divination.* New York: Penguin, 2005.

Pollack, Rachel. *The New Tarot Handbook.* Woodbury, MN: Llewellyn, 2011.

———. *Tarot Wisdom: Spiritual Teachings and Deeper Meanings.* Woodbury, MN: Llewellyn, 2008.

Thierens, A. E., and Arthur Edward Waite. *General Book of the Tarot.* White-
fish, MT: Kessinger Publishing, 2003.

Waite, Arthur Edward. *The Pictorial Key to the Tarot.* Stamford, CT: US Games,
1995.

Warwick-Smith, Kate. *The Tarot Court Cards: Archetypal Patterns of Relationship in the Minor Arcana.* Rochester, VT: Destiny Books, 2003.

Wirth, Oswald. *The Tarot of the Magicians.* Trans. Samuel Weiser, Inc. York
Beach, ME: Red Wheel/Weiser, 1985.

ABOUT THE AUTHOR

Courtney Weber is a Wiccan priestess, writer, tarot adviser, and activist. A tarot reader with nearly twenty years' experience, Courtney produced and designed Tarot of the Boroughs, a modern tarot deck set in New York City, composed of original photography. She is the author of *Brigid: History, Mystery, and Magick of the Celtic Goddess* (Weiser, 2015). She has been published on *The Huffington Post*, *The Wild Hunt*, in *Circle Times* magazine, and elsewhere.

Visit her at *www.thecocowitch.com*.

Photo by Rebekah Carmichael

TO OUR READERS